Internships in Foreign and Defense Policy

Internships in Foreign and Defense Policy

A Complete Guide for Women (& Men)

Prepared by

Women In International Security

A Project of the

Center for International Security Studies at Maryland

Seven Locks Press
Cabin John, MD/Washington, DC

Library of Congress Cataloging-in-Publication Data

Internships in foreign & defense policy: a complete guide for women
(& men) / prepared by Women In International Security.
p. cm.
ISBN 0-932020-75-5: $10.95
1. International relations—Study and teaching (Internship)-
United States—Directories. 2 Security, International—Study and
teaching (Internship)—United States—Directories. 3 Military
policy—Study and teaching (Internship)—United States—Directories.
I. Women in International Security (Project)
JX1293.U6I58 1990
353.0089'07—dc20 89-48298
CIP

Manufactured in the United States of America
Design and typeset by Robert Rand
Cover design by New Age Graphics
Printed by McNaughton & Gunn, Saline, MI

Printed on acid-free paper

For more information:
Seven Locks Press
P.O. Box 27
Cabin John, MD 20818
(301) 320-2130

Women In International Security

The United States faces a multitude of foreign policy challenges, and experienced and talented individuals drawn from all areas of national life must be available if wise choices are to be made. Yet in the past, women have not generally been among those asked to contribute their skills. In effect, 50 percent of the available talent has been excluded from the pool of individuals who will deal with the most vital issues facing us today.

But there are some positive signs. In the last 10 years, the percentage of doctorates awarded to women in international relations has doubled, and during the last 2 years, about a third of those entering the U.S. diplomatic corps have been women. More women are entering the graduate schools and professional programs that lead to effective membership in the policy community. The next few years will be critical if women are to advance to influential policy-making and research positions in significant numbers.

The Women In International Security project is a national, nonpartisan network and professional development program dedicated to enhancing the career prospects of women working in the field of international security. The program involves women in the military, in government, in policy-making and diplomatic areas, in the media, and in academia.

WIIS (pronounced "wise") is designed to enable women to fulfill their career expectations. We hope not only to increase the number of women working as international security professionals but also to enhance the prospects of those already in the field, especially at beginning and midcareer levels. WIIS provides women currently working in international security, as well as those considering it as a career, with a structure of informal links and continuing career contacts. This rests on a foundation of specific activities, including

- WIIS databank—a computerized listing that is used to match women and professional opportunities.
- WIIS directories—of which, this is the first; future ones will cover midcareer opportunities and other organizations and resources.
- *WIIS Words*—a quarterly newsletter.
- WIIS seminars—meetings that present networking opportunities and substantive discussions.

Women In International Security is funded by the Ford Foundation and a generous anonymous donor. Created in July 1987, it is run under the auspices of the Center for International Security Studies at Maryland, directed by Catherine McArdle Kelleher. The Center is located at the School of Public Affairs on the College Park campus of the University of Maryland. The executive director of WIIS is Frances G. Burwell, who can be reached at WIIS/CISSM, Morrill Hall, University of Maryland, College Park, MD 20742 (telephone: 301/454-5057).

Center for International Security Studies at Maryland

The Center for International Security Studies at Maryland, directed by Catherine McArdle Kelleher, is a nonpartisan organization dedicated to interdisciplinary research, education, and publication in the field of international security and foreign policy. Formerly called the Maryland International Security Project, CISSM was founded in 1984. Through disinterested analysis and promotion of postgraduate education and training, CISSM is working toward finding solutions to the intricate and dangerous problems of a world characterized by both economic interdependence and weapons of great destructive capability. Current collaborative projects include economics and national security, the history of nuclear weapons, Alliance relations, and ethics and national security, as well as women and international security.

For more information, contact the Director, Center for International Security Studies at Maryland, 3106 Morrill Hall, University of Maryland, College Park, MD 20742; or telephone (301) 454-4344.

Table Of Contents

Acknowledgments

This directory would not have been possible without the support and assistance of many individuals and institutions. Numerous graduate students at the University of Maryland contributed their time and effort, along with many suggestions as to what would make this directory most relevant. In particular, MacArthur Scholar Linda Staheli and Cathleen Corr of the School of Public Affairs spent hours on the phone and hunched over computer terminals as they collected, compiled, checked, and updated information on the many organizations listed. Linda also contributed significantly to the internship section. In the summer before starting Harvard University, Yvette Austin prepared the first draft of the annotated bibliography; our thanks to her and to Sandy Shmookler, who originally enlisted Yvette for WIIS. Lisa McAnany, a graduate student and MacArthur Scholar at Maryland's Department of Government and Politics, made significant additions to the bibliography, besides filling gaps throughout the entire directory. Dorothy H. Totz, editor for the Center for International Security Studies at Maryland, went through the entire manuscript, adding clarity and consistency to our often cumbersome prose. She also shepherded the manuscript through a complicated publications process.

Many others not directly involved in the production still contributed significantly to its existence and completion. Foremost among these is Dr. Catherine McArdle Kelleher, CISSM director. As the founder of the Women In International Security project, she is perhaps the person most responsible for the idea of such a directory. Many of the students, staff, and faculty affiliated with CISSM have been supportive of the WIIS project, and of the directory in particular, even when WIIS staff were monopolizing both the computer printer and copy machine. As part of CISSM, the WIIS project is associated with the University of Maryland's School of Public Affairs, whose dean, Michael Nacht, and the other faculty and staff provide hospitable surroundings. Students of the school have given encouragement in the most direct way by borrowing draft copies of the directory to assist in their own job searches.

In addition, thanks are due to many individuals and institutions outside the University of Maryland. Members of both the Board of Directors and the Advisory Board have been essential to the development of the WIIS program; their suggestions and counsel at critical junctures have helped immensely in the directory's development. The John D. and Catherine T. MacArthur Foundation, by providing financial support to CISSM for student fellowships, supplied essential assistance to the WIIS internship directory; in particular, both Linda Staheli and Lisa McAnany were supported by funds from a MacArthur Foundation institutional grant to CISSM while working on the directory. Finally, no acknowledgment would be complete without extending a heartfelt thanks to the Ford Foundation. It not only provided funds for the production of the directory itself, but without the Ford Foundation's generous support, the entire WIIS program would never have become a reality.

Frances G. Burwell
Executive Director

Women In International Security

ADVISORY BOARD

BOARD OF DIRECTORS

Preface

Women In International Security is an organization dedicated to supporting women in the traditionally male-dominated areas of foreign and defense policy. Its aims—among others—are to encourage more women to enter the field and to assist them in launching their careers. Successful careers require hard work, knowledge, and skills. But they also require contacts and a willingness to take advantage of opportunities. An internship early in a career can help an individual gain all of these.

As a women's group, WIIS feels there is a particular need for an internship directory especially directed toward women (of course, internships are valuable experiences for both men and women). While many legal obstacles to women's participation in the work force have fallen, many subtle barriers remain. Women, for example, may have to be especially well-informed and competent to be accepted as knowledgeable in their field. Often very qualified women are overlooked when speaking invitations and other valuable professional opportunities are brought up. This in turn makes it difficult to develop the credentials and public profile that can lead to promotion. Moreover, women—especially those just starting their careers—are often unaware of informal networks, rules, and procedures that may be important in a particular office or group. They may also find it difficult to develop a relationship with a mentor to explain this system, particularly if the pool of potential mentors is largely comprised of disinterested men.

Internships provide an opportunity to address these challenges. And, because the work environment for interns is usually relaxed, with everyone involved acknowledging the need for guidance, it is often easier to get some informal career counseling.

Internships in Foreign and Defense Policy lists approximately 80 organizations offering internships in the field of international security. While "international security" means different things to different people, states, and nations, for the purposes of this directory, WIIS has focused primarily on those institutions and organizations that are concerned with military or defense matters, foreign policy, and national policy and budget issues. An annotated bibliography is included that describes other directories that cover broader subject areas. Most of the organizations listed are located in or near Washington, DC, but there are also a number located in New York, Boston, and Atlanta.

It is the hope of all those who have contributed to the directory—WIIS staff, sponsoring organizations, and publisher—that this book will fulfill its twin goals of providing useful and up-to-date information about a variety of organizations, and that it will encourage women to explore the field of international security. While the competition for internships in this area is stiff, particularly in the nation's capital, the opportunities are abundant. With hard work and perseverance, individuals should be able to find an opening to provide the practical experience that will be so valuable later. For further information on WIIS, please contact us. We would also like your comments or suggestions. Good luck!

Women In International Security

ONE

Why Do an Internship?

Every summer, thousands of college students—both graduates and undergraduates—come to Washington. They spend two to three months working as interns for the government, nonprofit groups, research institutes, and a myriad of other types of organizations. Students range from art-history majors working for museum curators, to science majors spending the summer at the Environmental Protection Agency, to international relations students working for members of Congress on the various foreign affairs committees. Their responsibilities range from filing and answering the phone to writing policy papers and briefing officials. Some are paid a small salary, some receive college credit, but the vast majority work for free.

Why do so many students spend a summer or a semester in this way—working long hours, doing more than their share of clerical work, receiving little remuneration? Because they recognize the internship experience for what it is: an investment in their future. In a competitive job market, a solid academic background may not be enough to land a good position after graduation. This is particularly true in the field of international security, where there are many more qualified individuals than there are openings. Getting some basic working and professional experience while still a student can make a real difference after graduation. Moreover, an internship may help a student find her own individual career niche. Narrowing your focus, recognizing your strengths and weaknesses, and firming up your goals are all integral parts of launching a successful career.

Internships provide opportunities to develop three basic types of expertise: substantive, procedural, and "people" expertise. Substantive expertise consists of knowledge about particular issues, such as U.S.-Soviet arms control negotiations or Arab-Israeli relations. Most students arrive in the nation's capital already familiar with several such issues, even if it is knowledge gained largely from books and magazines. An internship provides an opportunity to supplement such secondary sources with firsthand information and perhaps even involvement in the issue itself.

Procedural expertise refers to an understanding of the policy process. This is in fact why most students come to Washington—"to see how policy is made." Most internships allow students to observe at close range how the different institutions—both in and out of government—operate; how organizations make decisions; and which groups have input at what point in the policy process. Such knowledge is often relevant in many areas and thus will be of benefit no matter what interests interns may pursue in the future.

People expertise, although a nebulous concept, should not be underestimated. It has two components: first, understanding how individuals operate in a professional environment, and what standards and behavior are expected for success; and, second, getting to know individuals and beginning to build a network of professional acquaintances. Having a group of people who think well of you and who are willing to work with you and recommend you to others is essential to a successful career. Internships offer excellent opportunities to identify such individuals and to demonstrate your talents through diligence and competence.

TWO

Finding an Internship in National Security

Finding the right internship will depend largely on how clearly you think through this search: What are your reasons for taking an internship? How much time and energy will you put into the process? Because of the ever-mounting competition, give yourself as much time as possible to locate a position, preferably six months at minimum. But before beginning, quiz yourself on the following questions:

- Why do I want an internship? What do I hope to gain through the experience: skills, contacts, or a better understanding of a particular area?
- What facet of national security interests me most: area studies, arms control, or strategic or military studies? (The more specific you are, the more credibility you convey in an interview.)
- What particular skills and talents do I bring? What are my strengths and weaknesses? Do I have experience that is of interest to this organization?
- Do I require supervision? What kind? Do I need a set agenda to follow or can I operate on my own? Am I a self-starter? Can I accept responsibility?
- What kind of office environment am I looking for? Do I prefer an office that is quiet and peaceful, maybe a research institute? Or do I like the hustle and bustle of a Capitol Hill office, or a frantic-paced editorial atmosphere?
- How much office work do I want to do? (Almost every internship has some clerical work, and a demonstrated willingness to do any task may lead to broader, more interesting responsibilities. However, no one wants to spend an entire internship at the copy machine, so be clear about the kind of substantive work you would like to do.)
- Can I afford to take a nonpaying internship? What expenses will I have, and how will I meet them? Do I have savings, financial aid, or other possibilities that would help cover the expenses of living?
- Do I prefer academic credit and/or some remuneration? How will this affect my internship search? Do I want to join an organized internship

program or arrange for credit on my own? To receive credit, do I need an academic adviser as a sponsor?
- When can I start the internship? When will I have to end it? Can I work full time or will I need to balance the internship with work or school?

BEGINNING THE SEARCH

With these basic questions confronted, you can now begin to peruse the listings. Don't range too far from your interests and background; after all, an organization concerned primarily with Latin America will probably not be interested in hiring you if your course work and research show a strong preference for U.S.-Soviet relations. At the same time, however, try to pursue as many leads as possible. Take a realistic view of your talents and how they could apply to particular organizations. Be willing to seek out opportunities, even where—at first glance—there seem to be none.

After identifying programs that interest you, first verify the information listed. Although every effort has been made to keep this directory up-to-date, changes are inevitable. Nonprofit organizations may be particularly susceptible to frequent shifts in staff and programs. If possible, call the organization to check its address; ask to speak to the internship coordinator (at the same time, identify yourself, giving your address). Confirm any deadlines and request that formal application materials be sent to you. This is also a good time to ask for general information, such as a brochure, on the organization itself. If, instead, you request this information in a letter, address it to the Internship Coordinator rather than to a particular person, unless you are sure of the individual's name.

It is best to apply well in advance of application deadlines. For summer internships for the federal government, deadlines might be as early as October 1 of the previous year. On the other hand, many nongovernmental organizations accept applications in March or April for the summer months.

GETTING THE RIGHT INTERNSHIP

Go over the application requirements and deadlines before preparing the necessary materials. If you already have a resume, it should be reviewed to make sure that it stresses the experience and skills that will make you attractive to the organizations to which you are applying. This may mean preparing two resumes—perhaps one for research-oriented work and another for more administrative positions; or one for a job that requires a general foreign policy analyst and another for an organization that would like the extensive work you have done on the Soviet Union, for example. Of course, all information on resumes should be accurate and truthful, but the way it is presented can make difference. It should highlight strengths and competencies. If you are unsure of the thrust of your resume, ask a friend to read it; getting other people's comments is usually instructive anyway. Don't neglect the basics of writing a resume: keep it on one page, if at all possible; check grammar and spelling; and use action words—such as *organized, wrote, coordinated,* and *implemented*—to describe the responsibilities you have had. (See sample resume on p. 95.)

A cover letter should go with the resume; use it to emphasize your strengths and how they relate to the specific organization and department. This is particularly important if you are unsure whether the resume adequately demonstrates your capability to fill the opening. Many organizations require additional material such as transcripts or writing samples. The latter should be relatively short—five pages or less—unless otherwise specified. Check all this material prior to deadlines. (See sample cover letter on p. 97.)

Almost all internships require letters of recommendation. These usually come from faculty members who are familiar with your academic work, but if there is someone from the business community who can attest to your abilities (your administrative skills, for example, or your independent motivation), it is worthwhile to include that recommendation as well. Make arrangements for the letters of recommendation early, so the individuals writing them have plenty of time. (See sample request for letter of recommendation on p. 99.)

After sending your materials, make a follow-up call to the internship coordinator one or two weeks later. Ask whether all the required materials have been received and what the process and timing will be for selecting the interns. This is also a good time to introduce yourself to the person heading the internship selection. It never hurts to say that you are greatly interested in working in this particular organization.

INTERVIEWS: WHAT TO EXPECT

If your qualifications and background meet the organization's needs, you may be called for an interview. Almost all positions entail an interview, even if simply done over the phone. However, it is to your advantage—and the organization's—to conduct a personal interview. It could take place somewhere mutually convenient with a representative of the organization; or it might require that you travel to the organization's office and talk with a member of the staff.

Many students interview for summer internships during spring break. If by then you have not been contacted, call the organization to ask whether you can visit and talk about internship possibilities. If you have applied to several places in Washington, for instance, you might be able to arrange a number of appointments over two or three days. Although these are not, in effect, job interviews, they do provide an opportunity for the internship coordinator and others to meet you personally. They also demonstrate your interest in the organization. Such a visit is especially helpful if your resume does not stand out from those of competitors.

An interview serves two purposes. First, it is an opportunity to get a better sense of the office atmosphere and the activities of the organization. Second, it is a chance for the people you may be working with to judge whether you have the expertise, background, and personality for the position. Personality, especially maturity and initiative, is an important factor; in many small nonprofit groups, interns may play a central, even responsible role. Thus, it is important to come across as competent, flexible, and cooperative, able to deal with whatever arises. The interview is a chance to sell yourself. One of the most effective ways to do this is to show your interest in the organization and its activities. Ask questions, and suggest ways that your past experiences might be relevant. Empathize with those making the final choice. You may have an excellent resume but if you don't communicate well, how will they determine whether your course work will translate effectively into the real-world environment? On the other hand, even with a less-than-perfect resume, if you can outline specific ways you can contribute to the organization, the position may be offered to you. After an interview, send a note to those with whom you talked, thanking them for their time and supplying any additional materials requested.

Finally, remember that looking for an internship—just like looking for a job—is a complex and time-consuming task. It pays to be persistent and organized. Keep all your materials in one place, and keep copies of all correspondence. Keep a list of the organizations and contact names, leaving enough space to update your progress. Note dates that you mailed the applications, received materials, etc. You may want to summarize conversations, and you should have a calendar with deadlines, reminding you when to make follow-up phone calls. With good organization, there is a greater likelihood of landing the position.

THE INFORMAL INTERNSHIP

Most internships listed in this directory are organized, existing programs. But many opportunities are created through an individual's initiative. Sometimes an office could use an intern but has not made the effort to find one. Or perhaps an organization may be looking for an intern but prefers to hire a person through its own casual network of contacts rather than through a formal selection procedure. After all, many regular jobs are never advertised but filled by word of mouth, and internships are not very different.

One intern describes finding her niche through the informal process: "As a graduate student, I came to Washington during my spring break knowing I wanted to work on a congressional committee over the summer. As far as I knew, the committee I was interested in was not formally seeking interns for the summer. With some homework, I got the names of key committee staff and set up some informal interviews. I found out that they could use some help and in no time I was working there over the summer. As it turned out, that internship was invaluable in helping me attain my current job."

To create an internship, it helps to develop ties to the network of individuals who hear about such opportunities. One way to do this is through "information interviews." Such meetings can provide knowledge about the field and contacts with individuals that may eventually lead to an internship. Getting an internship is often a matter of being the right person in the right place at the right time. The more people in the field who know you and that you want an internship, the more likely you will be that "right person."

For example, if you are interested in an internship within the arms control area, target organizations that work in that field, whether or not they have formal internship programs. Get in touch with a staff member either by phone or a letter. If choosing the latter method, write that you are looking for an internship and would appreciate a chance to meet and discuss the field in general and any opportunities that exist; enclose your resume. A few days later, call to set up an appointment. Most people will take the time to help beginners in the field, but be as flexible as possible regarding appointment days and hours. Get as much information as you can on the organization prior to the interview, and prepare specific questions.

Each interview should provide some additional knowledge or insight about an organization or the profession in general. It should also provide the names of other contacts in your search for an internship. With luck, the interviewer will discuss any future needs for interns the organization might have and at the same time suggest several others to whom you should talk. Do not be afraid to ask for names, and if it is appropriate, ask if you may mention this interview when contacting others.

Always follow up an interview with a brief, polite thank-you note. If you land an internship or job with contacts gleaned from an informational interview, it is good practice to send a note to that effect with additional thanks.

Locating an internship through informational interviewing can be a challenging, sometimes discouraging process. It is doubly difficult to do from a college campus halfway across the country. But this method can provide you with information about a range of organizations and with a list of contacts that could be of value throughout your professional life.

FUNDING YOUR INTERNSHIP

That most internships are unfunded is unfortunate but true. Moreover, living in a city such as Washington, even in a group house, is not cheap. As a result, many students who must earn money for tuition expenses do not consider an internship a realistic possibility, even though it may help them get a good job after graduation. Even those students who are lucky enough to get one of the few paid positions soon discover that additional income is necessary.

One source of funding for those seeking internships with organizations working on the issues of peace, disarmament, or nuclear arms control is the Herbert Scoville Jr. Peace Fellowship. Scoville Fellows serve as special project assistants on the staff of a participating nonprofit group in Washington, DC. A stipend of $1,200 per month is provided, and the duration of the fellowship ranges from four to six months. Applicants must be U.S. citizens and have an undergraduate degree; preference is given to those without substantial Washington experience. The deadline for the spring semester is October 15; for the fall semester, March 15. For applications and further information, contact the Scoville Peace Fellowship Program, 110 Maryland Avenue NE, Room 211, Washington, DC 20002 (telephone: 202/543-4100).

While there is little official financial support for interns, some universities and colleges do have scholarship funds; check at your home institution. Others may help to keep costs down by finding free lodging through alumni and other assistance.

In most cases, however, be prepared to be self-sufficient. While you will find plenty of other poverty-stricken interns with whom to commiserate, the sensible solution is to quickly find a paying job, perhaps at a restaurant or in a retail store. Because the internship usually takes up the normal business week, you will need to find work that doesn't infringe on your primary responsibilities. Most intern supervisors are well aware of the need to earn money and thus are tolerant when a student must leave for the paying job that makes the internship possible. Try to negotiate with the internship organization from the beginning, so that your hours could be flexible enough to accommodate a paying job. In some cases, working 30 hours a week as an intern and 20-30 more for pay somewhere else just might do it.

Holding a second job is not easy, however. Besides requiring working long hours, it may impede your ability to get the most out of the internship. And if all spare time is taken up by the need to earn money, it is impossible to exploit the internship to the fullest. In some offices, staffers—including unpaid interns—are expected to work late on occasion; your participation is part of doing your share. Moreover, there are many after-work events, such as receptions, lectures, and seminars, which can provide valuable opportunities for making contacts and enhancing substantive expertise.

There is no denying that an internship can be an expensive undertaking. If your costs can be covered, however, it is well worth it. Internships are valuable investments.

GETTING THE MOST OUT OF YOUR INTERNSHIP

Before you start your internship, think carefully and specifically about your goals. Most likely, you are aiming, among other things:

- To increase your knowledge about one or more substantive issues;
- To gain insights into the policy process; and
- To make contacts in a field where you may soon be job hunting.

Inevitably, these goals may conflict, simply because there are limits on your time and energy. Only you can really choose which should receive top priority; however, it is worth remembering that internships usually offer unusual opportunities to observe the policy process and meet people actively involved in the field. Spending the summer in the library may improve your knowledge about an issue, but you will gain just as much, even more, through participating in interviews, briefings, and other activities.

Be serious about your work—after all, your first priority is to do a good job—but a really successful internship includes activities outside the office as well. Whenever possible, take advantage of seminars, lectures, and other chances to observe and learn about organizational processes. Go out of your way to meet people wherever you work—peers as well as staff. One of the best sources of contacts is other interns. Almost inevitably, interns socialize primarily with other interns. Those who stay in the field will find themselves constantly crossing paths with fellow interns throughout their careers.

Succeeding in an internship is not simply a matter of deciding what you want to do or whom you want to meet, however. Before starting, discuss your duties with your supervisor to have a clear understanding of your responsibilities. Inevitably, they will include some clerical tasks; having a positive attitude from the beginning regardless of the assignment will make everyone grateful for your presence. After all, it is only natural that the new, temporary employee—the intern—be given the jobs the regular staffers will shun, if possible. In truth, they have all "paid their dues" at the copy machine already. It is most unlikely you will have access to a secretary; be prepared to do your own typing, and become familiar with the office computer system as soon as possible.

On the other hand, you shouldn't spend your entire summer doing clerical work. Get involved with the substantive work of the office immediately. If you are not assigned a task, discuss the various projects with staff members and volunteer to help. The best of situations is to have responsibility for a particular project, something tangible that will be produced at the end of your stay. This might be researching and writing a report, organizing a conference, or setting up a particular program. At summer's end you should have a specific and significant accomplishment to which you can refer in future resumes or job applications. Keep a list also of other tasks and accomplishments.

During your internship you will be working in a professional environment. To succeed, you need to be credible as a professional staff member, both within your organization and especially when representing it to others. Unlike student hours, work hours may not be flexible; it is necessary to conform to the usual starting and finishing times of your organization. If you are out of the office, make sure someone knows where you are and when you will return. Somewhat informal dress is acceptable among interns—after all, you cannot be expected to purchase an entire wardrobe for the summer—but do appear and behave in as professional a manner as possible.

At the end of the internship, you can consider your time well spent if you have increased your understanding of the policy process or a particular issue, and if you have started to develop a set of contacts in what may be your future profession. Remember that the end of an internship is often the beginning of a career. Many individuals now working as professionals in the field of international security started as interns, and WIIS encourages you to follow in their footsteps.

THREE

The Internships

The following pages provide a comprehensive description of the internship opportunities offered by approximately 80 organizations active in the field of national security. However, since many organizations not listed here occasionally sponsor interns even though they do not have an established, formal program with deadlines and definite qualifications, it is worthwhile to seek out other organizations on the chance that a visit might result in an accidental internship. Thus, the information presented here should not be regarded as the last word. Students interested in a particular organization should make inquiries even if the application deadline is past or the group is not included here. At worst you may receive a standard rejection letter; on the other hand, you might receive information about other opportunities or even an internship!

One organization not listed that does take interns—hundreds, perhaps thousands, every year—is the U.S. Congress. At times it seems like almost everyone in the international security field has worked in a congressional office at some point. Yet there is no formal comprehensive program. Internship applications must be filled out separately—office by office, committee by committee, and member by member. There are usually hordes of applicants, and competition is tough. A good strategy is to start with your own representatives and senators; they are not obligated to give you a job simply because you are a constituent, but you may find their aides more willing to listen to you and provide advice. Certainly, a would-be intern should apply to committees working on issues that are of special interest, but it is a good idea to apply also to individual representatives and senators on such committees. (For additional information on congressional internships, see the entry for *Internships and Fellowships: Congressional, Federal, and Other Work Experience Opportunities,* listed in the section on "Internship Directories.")

In short, finding an internship on Capitol Hill, as anywhere else, takes a good resume, recommendations, and skills, but it also involves persistence and some luck. We at WIIS hope the listings that follow will be helpful, but they are just a starting point.

ACCESS: A Security Information Service

1730 M Street NW, Suite 605
Washington, DC 20036
(202) 785-6630

Organization Type and Purpose

ACCESS is a nonprofit, nonpartisan information clearinghouse on international security and peace. Its purpose is to facilitate a better understanding of war, peace, and international security through impartial information programs and improved communication.

Internships

Internships are offered in several areas, including inquiry services, outreach publications, and special projects. The inquiry service directs persons seeking information to the most appropriate sources covering a range of views. Publications include the *Resource Brief* and *Security Spectrum;* both provide overviews of various perspectives on security issues. Applicants whose interests or expertise are in research, public relations, computer database management, information management, or other topics may tailor their internship to focus on specific areas.

Qualifications

Applicants should have some background in security/foreign policy affairs and possess good communication skills and some computer experience. Qualifications vary according to internship interest. Previous office experience is highly desirable.

Internship Dates and Duration

A minimum commitment of 10 weeks is usually required. Full- and part-time internships are available.

Funding/Academic Credit

Interns receive $50 per week. Academic credit may be arranged with schools and universities. Contact ACCESS for deadlines.

To Apply

Send a resume and letter of interest. Selected candidates will be asked to complete an internship application form and to submit a brief writing sample.

Women at ACCESS

Five out of seven full-time staff members are women, as are four out of the nine members of the board of directors.

Contact Person

Jill Ament, Internship Coordinator; ACCESS, 1730 M Street NW, Suite 605, Washington, DC 20036; (202) 785-6630.

American Association for the Advancement of Science Committee on Science, Arms Control, and National Security

1333 H Street NW
Washington, DC 20005
(202) 326-6490

Organization Type and Purpose

The Committee on Science, Arms Control, and National Security—a nonprofit group—focuses the scientific, technical, and organizational resources of the AAAS on effective approaches toward conflict resolution, control of nuclear weapons, and the improvement of national security. The AAAS council has passed resolutions that support arms control and the negotiation of a comprehensive test-ban treaty. The group opposes first-strike weapons and efforts that are inconsistent with the ABM Treaty.

Internships

The internship program provides students with an opportunity to participate in AAAS national security and arms control education projects. Duties involve helping organize annual symposia, congressional seminars, and workshops; performing background research; and assisting with publications.

Qualifications

Interns must be either graduate or undergraduate students but should have successfully completed at least two years' college training, including some course work in areas broadly relevant to the program. Applicants should be flexible and willing to work and learn in a nonacademic setting. Good communication skills are required.

Internship Dates and Duration

Internships are available on a semester and trimester basis, sometimes for longer periods.

Funding/Academic Credit

A modest stipend is usually associated with the internships.

To Apply

Send a resume, a writing sample relevant to the subject area, a statement of internship objectives, and the names of two references. Deadlines: for fall, June 15; for spring, October 15; for summer, March 15.

Women at AAAS:

No information provided.

Contact Person

Elizabeth Kirk, Program Head; American Association for the Advancement of Science, 1333 H Street NW, Washington, DC 20005; (202) 326-6490.

American Committee on U.S.-Soviet Relations

109 11th Street SE
Washington, DC 20003
(202) 546-1700

Organization Type and Purpose

As a nonprofit research group, the committee's focus is on independent, nonpartisan, educational efforts through programs and publications. Its aim is to strengthen official and public understanding of the complex overall relationship between the United States and the Soviet Union. Membership of the American Committee, composed of some 500 Republicans, Democrats, and independents, includes many of the key people involved in U.S.-Soviet relations since 1945. The committee publishes a bimonthly newsletter, *Outlook,* to inform and educate membership.

Internships

Interns assist the research staff on projects dealing with all aspects of the U. S.-Soviet relationship. Occasionally, interns assist in organizing conferences and meetings with prominent American and Soviet officials and scholars.

Qualifications

A strong background in Soviet studies and Russian language is preferred. Interns must be undergraduate or recent graduate students.

Internship Dates and Duration

Mostly during the fall, spring, or summer semesters, although flexibility is permitted.

Funding/Academic Credit

Stipends are occasionally offered. Academic credit is frequently available through the intern's home institution.

To Apply

Submit a letter, enclosing one recommendation, college transcript, and a writing sample of five to ten pages.

Women at the American Committee on U. S.-Soviet Relations

Approximately 50 percent of staff are women.

Contact Person

Mary Lee Grogan, Intern Coordinator; American Committee on U.S.-Soviet Relations, 109 11th Street SE, Washington, DC 20003; (202) 546-1700.

American Defense Institute

214 Massachusetts Avenue NE
Washington, DC 20013-2497
(202) 544-4704

Organization Type and Purpose

ADI, a nonprofit educational organization, works on national security issues with a special emphasis on educating young Americans about the need for a strong defense. Programs include a nationwide grass-roots campaign, a worldwide military-voter registration drive, and a national speakers bureau.

Internships

Duties include drafting letters and position statements for newsletters and other projects, conducting research (involves reading and attending congressional committee hearings), and planning a National Security Leadership Seminar for Capitol Hill interns. Occasional clerical duties are required. Interns can conduct research on the defense budget, SDI and arms control, NATO and Alliance policy, Soviet foreign policy, and various other security issues.

Qualifications

Interns must be juniors or seniors enrolled in a college or university pursuing a course of study in one of the following areas: political science, history, international relations, international law, or economics. Candidates should be creative and articulate and have excellent writing skills.

Internship Dates and Duration

Applications accepted on a year-round basis. Duration of internship varies.

Funding/Academic Credit

No information available.

To Apply

Write or call ADI for an application. After completion, send it with an official academic transcript and letters of recommendation to the contact person.

Women at the American Defense Institute

Seventy-five percent of staff are women.

Contact Person

Caroline Cahill, Program Director; American Defense Institute, 214 Massachusetts Avenue NE, Washington, DC 20013-2497; (202) 544-4704.

American Enterprise Institute for Public Policy

1150 17th Street NW
Washington, DC 20036
(202) 862-7182

Organization Type and Purpose

A nonprofit research institution, AEI studies current domestic and international issues. It produces the quarterly AEI *Foreign Policy and Defense Review* and houses the Center for Hemispheric Studies.

Internships

Information on specific duties of interns is not available, since it depends on the particular project to which the individual is assigned.

Qualifications

Applicants must be graduate or undergraduate students.

Internship Dates and Duration

Internships are scheduled for the fall, spring, and summer.

Funding/Academic Credit

Summer interns receive a stipend.

To Apply

Contact the AEI internship director.

Women at AEI

Information not available.

Contact Person

Christina Theberge, Internship Director; American Enterprise Institute for Public Policy, 1150 17th Street NW, Washington, DC 20036; (202) 862-7182.

American Friends Service Committee

1501 Cherry Street
Philadelphia, PA 19102
(215) 241-7111

Organization Type and Purpose

American Friends Service Committee is a humanitarian Quaker organization; it received the Nobel Prize in 1947 for "silent help from the nameless to the nameless." This nonprofit, educational group seeks to address social and economic inequalities and promote global peace. Recent projects include a peace-education project on disarmament and apartheid. Approximately 375 staff members work in the national office and in the nine regional offices in this country. Overseas bases in Africa, Latin America, and the Middle East employ 25 persons.

Internships

Undergraduate and graduate students may apply for U.S.-based internships, which are developed on an individual basis. Responsibilities include program research and office work. The committee also sponsors a community service program in Mexico.

Qualifications

Background should include previous experience in areas of AFSC programs and the ability to work independently.

Internship Dates and Duration

No information.

Funding/Academic Credit

Unpaid.

To Apply

Contact internship recruitment division.

Women at AFSC

No information available.

Contact Person

Lydia Wilcox, Personnel Department; American Friends Service Committee, 1501 Cherry Street, Philadelphia, PA 19102; (215) 241-7111.

American-Mideast Educational and Training Service

1100 17th Street NW
Suite 300
Washington, DC 20036
(202) 785-0022

Organization Type and Purpose

AMIDEAST, a nonprofit organization, works to develop human resources in the Middle East and North Africa and to promote understanding between the Arab world and the United States. These objectives are carried out through various U.S. and international programs.

Internships

Duties involve research, writing, and clerical and computer work.

Qualifications

Undergraduate and graduate students may apply.

Internship Dates and Duration

Internships are available throughout the year, including summer.

Funding/Academic Credit

Unpaid.

To Apply

Contact the internship coordinator.

Women at AMIDEAST

No information available.

Contact Person

Mary Didon, Director of Administration and Personnel; American-Mideast Educational and Training Service, 1100 17th Street NW, Suite 300, Washington, DC 20036; (202) 785-0022.

American Security Council

499 South Capitol Street SW
Suite 500
Washington, DC 20003
(202) 484-1676

Organization Type and Purpose

This organization is a nonprofit, research and interest group that works with other educational institutions to improve public understanding of national security issues. A prodefense citizen's group, it serves as the educational coordinator of the Coalition for Peace Through Strength. The coalition, which includes 250 members of Congress and 169 national organizations, is a bipartisan alliance of prodefense leaders who support the adoption of a national policy of peace-through-strength.

Internships

Interns research council projects, communicate with political action committees, write reports, help write radio actualities, and do clerical tasks. Projects focus on the production of national security reports and the annual Voting Index. Interns are likely to meet a number of officials from Congress, the Defense Department, and the State Department.

Qualifications

Undergraduate and graduate students may apply; a knowledge of Spanish is helpful but not required.

Internship Dates and Duration

Two internships are offered each academic semester and the summer session.

Funding/Academic Credit

Interns receive a daily stipend of $20. One course credit per internship is granted. Deadlines: for summer, April 15; for fall, August 15; for spring, December 1.

To Apply

Submit writing samples and a cover letter to the American Security Council.

Women at the Council

No information available.

Contact Person

Greg Hilton, Intern Coordinator; American Security Council, 499 South Capitol Street SW, Suite 500, Washington DC 20003; (202) 484-1676.

Americas Society, Inc.

680 Park Avenue
New York, NY 10021
(212) 628-3200

Organization Type and Purpose

This private, nonprofit educational organization seeks to promote an understanding of the economic, political, and cultural values of Latin America, the Caribbean, and Canada through various programs and services.

Internships

Three to five unpaid internships are offered in its Latin American department. Interns deal with journalists, handle public relations work, assist with clerical tasks, organize luncheons, and assist visiting leaders from Latin America.

Qualifications

Applicants should be undergraduates or M.A. or Ph.D. candidates in international or Latin American affairs.

Internship Dates and Duration

Internships are available in the fall, spring, and summer.

Funding/Academic Credit

Internships are unpaid, but graduate credit may be arranged.

To Apply

No formal deadline. Contact the director of Latin American affairs.

Women at the Americas Society

No information available.

Contact Person

Ivan Rebolledo, Director; Americas Society, Inc., 680 Park Avenue, New York, NY 10021; (212) 628-3200.

Amnesty International USA

608 Massachusetts Avenue NE
Washington, DC 20002
(202) 547-4718

Organization Type and Purpose

Amnesty International is a worldwide, nonprofit human-rights movement. It works impartially for the release of prisoners of conscience, for fair trials, for political prisoners, and for an end to torture and executions. The Mid-Atlantic regional office organizes efforts on state and regional levels, membership development and outreach fund-raising, and grass-roots work. The Washington office focuses on influencing legislation on Capitol Hill, monitoring hearings, compiling reports, and attending meetings.

Internships

Student internships provide a hands-on opportunity to gain an in-depth understanding of the international human-rights field and the specific role that Amnesty plays. Clerical tasks involve at most 20 percent of responsibilities.

Qualifications

Applicants should be able to work cooperatively as well as independently when necessary. Good written and verbal communication skills are required. A familiarity with Amnesty's work, organizing skills, and computer experience is helpful, as is a knowledge of world affairs.

Internship Dates and Duration

Assignments generally cover an academic semester, two to five days a week.

Funding/Academic Credit

All internships are unpaid.

To Apply

Students should apply as soon as possible due to demand. Send a resume and cover letter expressing interest, the number of days per week available, and the dates possible to begin the internship. Also send a writing sample and two letters of recommendation; personal interviews are welcome.

Women at Amnesty

Seventy-five percent of the staff are women; the percentage of women interns varies.

Contact Person

Courtney Thompson, Intern Coordinator; Amnesty International USA, 608 Massachusetts Avenue NE, Washington, DC 20002; (202) 547-4718.

Arms Control and Foreign Policy Caucus

501 House Annex 2
Washington, DC 20515
(202) 226-3440

Organization Type and Purpose

This bipartisan group of 120 like-minded legislators (representatives and senators) is concerned with foreign policy and arms control research. Members receive publications, fact sheets, and a weekly committee schedule.

Internships

The caucus usually accepts three to four interns a semester. Duties include assisting staff with arms control and foreign policy projects and doing background research for caucus legislative bulletins. Past projects include researching potential congressional hurdles facing INF treaty ratification, monitoring aid to El Salvador, and tracking the Central American peace process. This is an opportunity to learn a great deal about both House and Senate procedures and about how Congress approaches arms control and foreign policy issues. The caucus is also a good place to intern before job hunting on the Hill.

Qualifications

An ability to write clearly and concisely and to meet fast-paced deadlines is essential. Applicants should also be interested in arms control and foreign policy issues and in congressional decision making in these areas. Attention to detail and accuracy is also important.

Internship Dates and Duration

Interns work full time, five days a week, for a minimum of three months.

Funding/Academic Credit

Unpaid. Academic credit arrangements can be made.

To Apply

Write for an application; include a resume, a two-page writing sample (preferably not an unfinished excerpt), and two recommendations. For the summer the deadline is March 1; otherwise, it is usually one month before starting.

Women at the Caucus

Of four staff members, three are women; one intern is usually a woman.

Contact Person

Margie Ellis, Internship Coordinator; Arms Control and Foreign Policy Caucus, 501 House Annex 2, Washington, DC 20515; (202) 226-3440.

Arms Control Association

11 Dupont Circle NW
Washington, DC 20036
(202) 797-6450

Organization Type and Purpose

ACA, a nonprofit educational organization, seeks to create broad public appreciation of the need for arms limitation as a means to enhance national security and promote world peace. The association publishes a monthly journal, *Arms Control Today*. ACA participates in press and public education programs and serves as a central clearinghouse for arms control information.

Internships

Interns assist staff analysts working on national security, defense, and arms control issues; help to prepare and edit *Arms Control Today;* monitor activity on Capitol Hill; and perform administrative tasks.

Qualifications

Internships are offered to undergraduates, graduates, and other individuals interested in arms control. Applicants should be interested in national security affairs and possess good writing and interpersonal skills and office experience. Substantive background is useful but less important than willingness to work hard and to learn.

Internship Dates and Duration

Internships are fairly flexible but generally run in the fall, winter, and summer.

Funding/Academic Credit

Unpaid.

To Apply

Send a resume, a brief writing sample, and other relevant material to the intern coordinator; personal interviews are strongly encouraged. Deadlines (apply early): for fall, August 31; for winter, January 31; for summer, April 15.

Women at the Arms Control Association

Information not available.

Contact Person

Felicia Wong, Intern Coordinator; Arms Control Association, 11 Dupont Circle NW, Washington, DC 20036; (202) 797-6450.

Asia Foundation

550 Kearny Street
San Francisco, CA 94108
(415) 982-4640

Organization Type and Purpose

The Asia Foundation sponsors a variety of programs throughout East and Southeast Asia. The educational, nonprofit foundation is particularly interested in fostering political development, constructive social change, equitable economic growth, and cooperative international relationships.

Internships

Interns work on ongoing projects. The program is coordinated with the formal internship program at the University of California at Berkeley.

Qualifications

Open to undergraduate and graduate students.

Internship Dates and Duration

Ad hoc internships are arranged generally during summer (this is especially true for non-Berkeley students), but internships can last for a one-year period.

Funding/Academic Credit

Berkeley students are reimbursed for a semester's tuition and transportation costs. Other interns usually receive a small stipend.

To Apply

Contact the director of personnel.

Women at the Asia Foundation

No information available.

Contact Person

G.K. LeRoy, Personnel Officer; Asia Foundation, 550 Kearny Street, San Francisco, CA 94108; (415) 982-4640.

Asia Society

725 Park Avenue
New York, NY 10021
(212) 288-6400

Organization Type and Purpose

The Asia Society was established in 1956 by John D. Rockefeller III to promote cross-cultural understanding between Asia and the United States. The society, which is educational and nonprofit, has regional offices in Washington, D.C., Houston, and Los Angeles. Of a professional staff of 56, 50 work in New York.

Internships

Responsibilities include some administrative chores and work on ongoing projects.

Qualifications

Undergraduate or graduate students may apply. An interest in Asian studies is helpful.

Internship Dates and Duration

Internships can be arranged for summer or for a 12-month period.

Funding/Academic Credit

Unpaid.

To Apply

Contact director of administration.

Women at the Asia Society

No information available.

Contact Person

Louise Wilson, Director of Administration; Asia Society, 725 Park Avenue, New York, NY 10021; (212) 288-6400.

Association to Unite the Democracies

1506 Pennsylvania Avenue SE
Washington, DC 20003
(202) 544-5150

Organization Type and Purpose

This nonprofit association supports existing movements for democracy and regional unification throughout the globe. It advocates the establishment of a world assembly of all democracies and works toward a federation of the Atlantic and Pacific allies as a means to ensure a safer world.

Internships

Internships concentrate on an agreed-upon project, such as research on a topic of mutual interest, or a project to advance an association goal or to disseminate its message.

Qualifications

Candidates should demonstrate interest in and a background relevant to the organization's goals.

Internship Dates and Duration

Flexible.

Funding/Academic Credit

AUD reimburses small expenses incurred during the internship.

To Apply

Send a resume and transcript with a letter indicating why you want to work with AUD.

Women at AUD

Two-fifths of the staff are women.

Contact Person

Ira Straus, Executive Director; Association to Unite the Democracies, 1506 Pennsylvania Avenue SE, Washington, DC 20003; (202) 544-5150.

Beijing-Washington Inc.

4340 East-West Highway
Suite 200
Bethesda, MD 20814
(301) 656-4801

Organization Type and Purpose

This consulting firm represents approximately 30 U.S., Canadian, and European companies in the People's Republic of China. Beijing-Washington concentrates on the marketing and sales of electronic equipment components and technology to China.

Internships

Duties are largely administrative at first, involving clerical work and word processing. Other responsibilities include assisting project managers with mass mailings, writing Chinese addresses, responding to requests from buyers and/or factories in China, and assisting with research projects.

Qualifications

An ability to write and speak Mandarin Chinese is required. In addition, applicants should have an active interest in developing commerce in China.

Internship Dates and Duration

Offered in the spring, fall, and summer; interns work about 16 hours per week for 10 weeks.

Funding/Academic Credit

Though unpaid, the internship could possibly develop into a full-time, paid position.

To Apply

No formal deadline. Send a resume, noting dates available, to the contact person.

Women at Beijing-Washington

No information available.

Contact Person

Patricia Sale, Assistant to the President; Beijing-Washington, Inc., 4340 East-West Highway, Suite 200, Bethesda, MD 20814; (301) 656-4801.

Business Executives for National Security

601 Pennsylvania Avenue NW
Suite 700
Washington, DC 20004-2602
(202) 737-1090

Organization Type and Purpose

BENS is a national, nonpartisan trade association comprised of 5,000 business leaders who offer practical suggestions about how to deal constructively with U.S. national security issues. The association takes a nonideological approach to America's security.

Internships

Candidates have an opportunity to work on crucial issues in national security. Internships are offered in three areas: communications, research, and resources.

Qualifications

Qualifications differ according to internship focus. Common requirements include excellent writing and typing skills, good interpersonal skills, and some faculty for working with computers. Candidates should be detail oriented, possess good phone manners, and have a desire to learn new skills. An interest in national security is preferred.

Internship Dates and Duration

Internships are offered year-round.

Funding/Academic Credit

A stipend of $150 per month is usually paid.

To Apply

Send a resume, a short writing sample (three to five pages), two letters of recommendation, and two references. Include a cover letter explaining which internship you are applying for, why you are interested in it, and how the position fits with career educational or personal goals (applicants may apply for more than one internship). Deadlines: summer, April 11; fall, August 1; winter/spring, December 1.

Women at BENS

There are 13 women on staff in the Washington office and 6 in the regional offices.

Contact Person

Matthew Patchell, Intern Coordinator; Business Executives for National Security, 601 Pennsylvania Avenue NW, Suite 700, Washington, DC 20004-2602; (202) 737-1090.

Carnegie Endowment for International Peace

11 Dupont Circle NW, Suite 900
Washington, DC 20036
(202) 797-6488

Organization Type and Purpose

The Carnegie Endowment, a nonprofit operating foundation, conducts its own programs of research, discussion, publication, and education in international affairs and U.S. foreign policy. The endowment publishes *Foreign Policy* and is associated with the Arms Control Association.

Internships

Unpaid internships are available during each academic semester and the summer. A stipend is offered for a six-month internship open only to graduating college seniors. Interns are assigned to *Foreign Policy*, the nuclear nonproliferation project, or the Office of the Secretary.

Qualifications

Candidates should have a background in international relations, political science, history, economics, or area studies. To receive the six-month internship (with stipend), students must be nominated by their college and have completed a significant amount of course work in international politics and economics.

Internship Dates and Duration

Volunteer positions are year-round. Paid student internships are for six months.

Funding/Academic Credit

Volunteers receive transportation costs; six-month, paid slots provide $1,300 per month, plus medical, life, and business-travel insurance.

To Apply

For paid internships, apply by January 15 for next academic year. For unpaid ones, apply August 1 for September; December, for January; April, for June. Volunteers should send a resume and cover letter stating hours per week available and dates of availability. For paid student interns, the following must be sent to the contact person by January 15: a statement of nomination from university contact, a one-page resume, two recommendations, transcripts, and an essay under five pages. Call or write for specifics.

Women at Carnegie

Approximately 50 percent of the staff and interns are women.

Contact Person

Jean Hensley, Manager for Personnel Services; Carnegie Endowment for International Peace, 11 Dupont Circle NW, Suite 900, Washington, DC 20036; (202) 797-6488.

Carter Center, Emory University

One Copenhill
Atlanta, GA 30307
(404)420-5151

Organization Type and Purpose

The center's primary objectives are to facilitate constructive dialogue between diplomats, scholars, business leaders, and other decision makers; to promote education based on scholarly research; and to implement outreach programs that can influence local and international public policies. Interns have the unique opportunity to come in contact with former president Jimmy Carter and other dignitaries. Carter cochairs conferences, meets with former and present heads of state, and participates in events sponsored by the fellows throughout the academic year.

Internships

Interns participate in the center's projects on human rights, international conflict resolution, Latin American and Caribbean studies, Middle Eastern studies, and U.S.-Soviet relations, as well as projects in the offices of development and public relations.

Qualifications

Candidates may be undergraduates or graduates. Qualifications differ depending on the project; contact the Carter Center for specifics.

Internship Dates and Duration

Internships are offered on a semester basis, year-round.

Funding/Academic Credit

Internships are unpaid.

To Apply

Contact the center for an application form.

Women at the Center

No information available.

Contact Person

Linda Helms, Education Coordinator; Carter Center, One Copenhill, Atlanta, GA 30307; (404) 420-5151.

Center for Defense Information

1500 Massachusetts Avenue NW
Washington, DC 20005
(202) 862-0700

Organization Type and Purpose

CDI is a nonprofit research organization that provides objective information and analyses relating to national defense and security to the public, the press, and governmental agencies. Research is usually oriented toward the publication of CDI's journal *Defense Monitor* and the weekly TV program "America's Defense Monitor."

Internships

Applicants must be undergraduates or graduates. Internships are available on a full-time basis. Interns focus two-thirds of their time on research and one-third on administrative duties.

Qualifications

A strong interest in both U.S. military issues and public policy questions is desired. Writing skills are essential. Prior course work in these areas is not required; however, high academic achievements are important.

Internship Dates and Duration

Internships are year-round: January to May; June to August; and September to December.

Funding/Academic Credit

A stipend of $600 per month is offered. Interns may earn academic credit or serve without compensation.

To Apply

Submit a resume, a writing sample, transcripts of college course work, at least two letters of recommendation, and a personal letter describing interests and goals. Deadlines: for fall, July 1; for spring, November 1; for summer, April 1.

Women at CDI

The staff is 33 percent women. Percentage of women interns ranges from 50 percent to 65 percent.

Contact Person

Sanford Gottlieb, Intern Program Coordinator; Center for Defense Information, 1500 Massachusetts Avenue NW, Washington, DC 20005; (202) 862-0700.

Center for International Policy

1755 Massachusetts Avenue NW
Suite 500
Washington, DC 20036
(202) 544-4666

Organization Type and Purpose

The nonprofit Center for International Policy is concerned with the impact of U.S. foreign policy on human rights and socioeconomic conditions in the Third World.

Internships

Interns attend hearings, meetings, and briefings; they also conduct research and write, and are responsible for general administrative duties.

Qualifications

Knowledge of Spanish is helpful but not required. Familiarity with Central American affairs and U.S. policy toward the region is of benefit. Good writing and research skills are mandatory.

Internship Dates and Duration

Ten-week commitment for summer, fall, winter, or spring months. Deadlines: for summer, March; for fall, July; for winter, September; for spring, December.

Funding/Academic Credit

Unpaid, however, credit can be arranged.

To Apply

Send a resume, cover letter, and short writing sample (under four pages) to CIP.

Women at CIP

Of the staff, 33 percent are women; of the interns, approximately 50 percent are women.

Contact Person

William Goodfellow, Director; Center for International Policy, 1755 Massachusetts Avenue NW, Suite 500, Washington, DC 20036; (202) 544-4666.

Center for National Security Studies

122 Maryland Avenue NE
Washington, DC 20002
(202) 544-1681

Organization Type and Purpose

The Center for National Security Studies, a nonprofit research group, publishes a wide variety of books and reports and a bimonthly newsletter, *First Principles,* on national security issues.

Internships

Undergraduate interns assist primarily with research and writing on both long- and short-term projects. Areas of interest include activities of the intelligence community, export control, covert operations, and human rights in Central America.

Qualifications

Applicants should show a strong interest in civil-liberties issues and the legislative process and a commitment to the former. Good writing and research skills are essential as is an ability to work independently. Some understanding of constitutional law and legal research is helpful but not required.

Internship Dates and Duration

Internships are offered full time during semesters throughout the year.

Funding/Academic Credit

Unpaid.

To Apply

Students with questions or who wish to apply should contact the internship coordinator. Decisions are made on the basis of resumes and writing samples. Deadline for summer: March 15.

Women at the Center

No information available.

Contact Person

Tamara Silver, Internship Coordinator; Center for National Security Studies, 122 Maryland Avenue NE, Washington, DC 20002; (202) 544-1681.

Center for Strategic and International Studies

1800 K Street NW
Suite 400
Washington, DC 20006
(202) 887-0200

Organization Type and Purpose

CSIS is a nonprofit, public-policy research organization. Its primary goals are to anticipate issues, predict crisis situations, and communicate research to legislators, academicians, and the general public.

Internships

CSIS hosts 125 interns throughout the year. Individual assignments vary but usually include research assistance in seminar coordination and liaison work with other agencies. Internships focus on regional studies, arms control, political-military affairs, and international affairs and may lead to employment with CSIS.

Qualifications

Candidates should be undergraduates or graduates with an interest/background in international affairs and a strong background in economics. Knowledge of foreign languages—especially French, Russian, or Spanish—is helpful but not required.

Internship Dates and Duration

Internships may be on a full- or part-time basis during the academic year.

Funding/Academic Credit

Unpaid.

To Apply

Applicants must send two copies of a current resume, a writing sample, and transcripts to the intern coordinator. A letter should outline interests, college course work, and availability. Personal interviews are encouraged but not always possible; a telephone interview will suffice. No formal deadline.

Women at CSIS

Approximately 50 percent of staff and 45 percent of interns are women.

Contact Person

Ann Tennison, Intern Coordinator; Center for Strategic and International Studies, 1800 K Street NW, Suite 400, Washington, DC 20006; (202) 887-0200.

Center for the Study of Foreign Affairs

1400 Key Boulevard
Rosslyn, VA 22209
(703) 235-2109

Organization Type and Purpose

The center endeavors to keep government officials abreast of emerging foreign policy concepts by hosting conferences, directing research, conducting diplomatic exercises and simulations, and publishing materials. The center is part of the Foreign Service Institute in the State Department.

Internships

Interns assist professional staff on conferences, publications, seminars, and simulations dealing with current foreign affairs topics. Responsibilities include research, writing, and clerical work; an ability to organize is helpful. Two to five internships are offered.

Qualifications

Previous interns have been graduate or advanced undergraduate students with academic backgrounds and sometimes work experience in foreign affairs. A security clearance is desirable. Interns are formally contracted to the State Department.

Internship Dates and Duration

Internships are available throughout the year; interns work about 20 hours a week.

Funding/Academic Credit

Salary is negotiable, approximately $8.00 per hour; no academic credit is available.

To Apply

Call the contact person.

Women at the Center

Currently two of three program assistants are women. Of an eight-person staff, one is a woman.

Contact Person

Dean Howells, Acting Director; Center for the Study of Foreign Affairs, 1400 Key Boulevard, Rosslyn, VA 22209; (703) 235-2109.

Central Intelligence Agency

Washington, DC 20505
(703) 351-2053

Organization Type and Purpose

This executive agency has primary responsibility for the clandestine collection of foreign intelligence, the conduct of counterintelligence abroad, and the research and development of technical collection systems. One of the largest federal agencies, it offers internationally related employment opportunities for persons of almost every background and academic discipline. The CIA has four directorates: intelligence, operations, science and technology, and administration.

Internships

The CIA participates in a co-op program for undergraduates as well as a graduate studies program in which most graduate students are placed (see "Special Internship Programs"). In a separate internship program, summer research and engineering opportunities are offered to graduate students in high-tech fields.

Qualifications

The co-op program is geared to undergraduates majoring in architecture, chemistry, computer science, engineering, geography, graphic design, logistics, management information systems, mathematics, non-Roman languages, personnel administration, and physics. Candidates must maintain a 2.75 GPA. Co-op students must work a minimum of three terms.

Internship Dates and Duration

The graduate studies program is offered in the summer.

Funding/Academic Credit

A stipend is offered.

To Apply

For the graduate studies program, send a resume and writing sample. Applications must be received by mid-November for the following summer.

Women at the CIA

Information not available.

Contact Person

Michael Turner, Coordinator for Academic Affairs; Central Intelligence Agency, Washington, DC 20505; (703) 351-2053.

Chicago Council on Foreign Relations

116 South Michigan Avenue
Chicago, IL 60603
(312) 726-3860

Organization Type and Purpose

The council promotes public education, conducts research, and issues publications on foreign policy topics. Its conference series provides a private forum for leaders to discuss important issues of foreign policy.

Internships

Internships are occasionally available to students.

Qualifications

Applicants sought are generally graduate students in public policy or international relations.

Internship Dates and Duration

Generally, internships take place during the academic year.

Funding/Academic Credit

No information available.

To Apply

Contact the vice president listed below.

Women at the Council

No information available.

Contact Person

Arthur Cyr, Vice President and Program Director; Chicago Council on Foreign Relations, 116 South Michigan Avenue, Chicago, IL 60603; (312) 726-3860.

Committee for National Security

1601 Connecticut Avenue NW
Suite 301
Washington, DC 20009
(202) 745-2450

Organization Type and Purpose

CNS is a nonprofit, nonpartisan organization that informs Americans about arms control and national security issues; it also encourages active citizen participation in the ongoing debate over U.S. military and foreign policy. The committee conducts an extensive public affairs program.

Internships

Internships focus on research, fieldwork, public affairs, U.S.-Soviet relations, marketing, administration, and women's outreach programs. Interns are also expected to assist with overall office tasks.

Qualifications

The qualifications differ somewhat depending on the area of interest. Generally, strong research, writing, and editing skills are required, especially for the research and press positions; organizational and personal skills for the field position; and strong marketing skills for the U.S.-Soviet and marketing program.

Internship Dates and Duration

Internships are offered on a semester basis. Interns are asked to work at least three days per week.

Funding/Academic Credit

No funding available.

To Apply

Submit a cover letter describing your interests and timetable, two letters of recommendation from current and former professors and employers, a resume, a recent writing sample, and a copy of your academic transcript. Apply at least six weeks prior to start of semester during which you can work. Preliminary interviews will be conducted by phone. Applicants may contact CNS for status of application.

Women at CNS

Of total staff, 80 percent are women; 60 percent of current interns are women.

Contact Person

Jessica Aberly, Administrative Assistant; Committee for National Security, 1601 Connecticut Avenue NW, Suite 301, Washington, DC 20009; (202) 745-2450.

Common Cause

2030 M Street NW
Washington, DC 20036
(202) 833-1200

Organization Type and Purpose

Common Cause is a 280,000-member nonprofit and nonpartisan citizens' lobby. It works to make government function in a more efficient, responsive, and honest manner. Current issues include campaign finance reform, nuclear arms control, and ethics in government.

Internships

Interns coordinate grass-roots lobbying efforts, contribute to policy papers and investigative studies, monitor congressional committee meetings, function as press office and administrative aides, and research articles for *Common Cause* magazine. Assignments are made on the basis of both students' interests and CC needs. Opportunities include working with administration issues, development, membership and media communications, legislation, the magazine, and as grass-roots organizers to mobilize and educate CC members nationwide.

Qualifications

Undergraduate and graduate students should have a public-interest commitment, strong writing skills, and an ability to work with a wide variety of people.

Internship Dates and Duration

Interns must work at least two full days per week for a 10- to 12- week period. Internships are offered during fall, spring, and summer semesters.

Funding/Academic Credit

Internships are not funded; however, transportation to and from work is reimbursed. Credit must be arranged by students and their college.

To Apply

Phone or write for a Common Cause intern application. Send the completed application with two letters of recommendation and a three-page (or longer) writing sample. A personal interview is desired but phone interviews are acceptable. Deadlines for spring/fall are open; for summer, April 1.

Women at Common Cause

Of the staff, 80 percent are women; 50 percent of interns are women.

Contact Person

Mike Brogioli, Volunteer Coordinator; Common Cause, 2030 M Street NW, Washington, DC 20036; (202) 833-1200.

Congressional Research Service

Library of Congress
Washington, DC 20540
(202) 707-7127

Organization Type and Purpose

CRS is a department of the Library of Congress. It provides nonpartisan research and reference assistance exclusively to Congress. Its foreign affairs and national defense division responds to congressional queries about foreign policy and military issues. Approximately 60 professionals work in this division; total CRS staff is 860.

Internships

CRS sponsors two types of internship programs. Foreign and defense policy research associate (FDPRA) positions are available for graduate students and those who have undergraduate degrees. The second internship program, the student volunteer program, places students throughout CRS depending on the needs of specific divisions.

Qualifications

For the FDPRA position, a B.A. with an emphasis on foreign or defense policy or the social sciences and at least three months' previous research or graduate training in related fields are required. Candidates must be nominated by their school or a policy research organization.

Internship Dates and Duration

FDPRA positions are available for three-month terms; volunteer positions are offered year-round.

Funding/Academic Credit

Research associate positions are funded. Rate of pay is comparable to a GS-5, or $15,188 per year. Remuneration varies according to season. Student volunteer program is unpaid.

To Apply

For the paid positions in foreign and defense policy, contact that division. For student volunteer program, contact Administrative Officer, Office of Management and Administrative Services, Room LM 208 (phone: 707-8803). For the volunteer program, students should send a Standard Form 171 with a cover letter, giving dates of availability.

Women at CRS

Women comprise 26 percent of permanent professional staff.

Contact Person

Leneice Wu, Coordinator of Division Research; Congressional Research Service, Foreign Affairs and National Defense Division, Library of Congress, Washington, DC 20540; (202) 707-7127.

Council for a Livable World

20 Park Plaza
Boston, MA 02116
(617) 542-2282

Washington Office:
100 Maryland Avenue NE
Washington, DC 20002
(202) 543-4100

Organization Type and Purpose

The council's primary activity is lobbying Congress—to persuade elected officials that strong legislative measures are needed to stop and reverse the nuclear arms race. This nonprofit, educational, and advocacy group is also the largest political action committee on arms control, having backed 35 current senators. The Washington office sponsors seminars, helps shape legislation, and informs the press and public on key issues. The council was founded in 1962 by the eminent nuclear physicist Leo Szilard and other scientists who worked in the pioneer days of nuclear weapons.

Internships

Interns take part in all aspects of CLW's work, from lobbying and devising strategies with other arms control groups to researching and drafting publications for dissemination to Congress, the press, and public. Some office tasks are required: for example, answering mail, handling telephone inquiries, and delivering literature to congressional offices.

Qualifications

An interest in and commitment to arms control is essential, as well as the ability to work independently and be a self-starter. Some academic experience and/or activist background is preferred.

Internship Dates and Duration

Internship period covers three to four months: January to April; May to August; September to December.

Funding/Academic Credit

Unpaid, but college credit may be arranged.

To Apply

Send a cover letter with resume, writing sample, and reference letter. Deadlines: spring, December 15; summer, April 15; fall, August 15.

Women at CLW

Approximately 50 percent of the staff are women; number of women interns varies.

Contact Person

Michelle Robinson, Internship Coordinator; Council for a Livable World, 100 Maryland Avenue NE, Washington, DC 20002; (202) 543-4100; in Boston, call (617) 542-2282.

Council on Economic Priorities

30 Irving Place
New York, NY 10003
(212) 420-1133

Organization Type and Purpose

The Council on Economic Priorities researches, collects, furnishes, and publicizes the facts behind corporate and governmental programs to reveal how they actually impact on people, progress, and profits. This nonprofit, educational organization also has projects relating to national security.

Internships

Duties include research on arms control issues, verification, and the economic implications and strategic advisability of the Strategic Defense Initiative. Interns also work on letter-writing projects, press and public relations, and fund-raising.

Qualifications

An interest in arms control is helpful. Personal computer experience is essential. Willingness to work under tight deadlines is important. Good communication skills and an ability to work independently and set priorities are also desired.

Internship Dates and Duration

Term required: three months; summer internships are full time. During academic year, however, part-time internships are permissible.

Funding/Academic Credit

Undergraduates receive $100 per week; graduates, $125 per week.

To Apply

Send resume to above address; phone or write for more information.

Women at CEP

Of the staff, 80 percent are women; percentage of women interns varies.

Contact Person

Sheila Ratner, Administrative Director; Council on Economic Priorities, 30 Irving Place, New York, NY 10003; (212) 420-1133.

Council on Foreign Relations

58 East 68th Street
New York, NY 10021
(212) 734-0400

Organization Type and Purpose

The council, an educational and research institute, brings together leaders from the academic, public, and private sectors. Its goals are to help shape American foreign policy and to provide continuing leadership for the conduct of U.S. foreign relations.

Internships

Interns work on *Foreign Affairs,* the council's quarterly journal.

Qualifications

The council offers internships to undergraduates and graduates with a background in journalism or English. Positions are very competitive, primarily filled by graduate students with international affairs credentials.

Internship Dates and Duration

Generally, the council accepts three interns a year, one each in the summer, fall, and spring.

Funding/Academic Credit

Only summer interns receive a stipend; fall and spring positions are not funded.

To Apply

Contact the person indicated below.

Women at the Council

Approximately 60 percent of the staff are women.

Contact Person

Linda Robinson, Associate Editor, *Foreign Affairs;* Council on Foreign Relations, 58 East 68th Street, New York, NY 10021; (212) 734-0400.

Defense Budget Project

236 Massachusetts Avenue NE
Suite 301
Washington, DC 20002
(202) 546-9737

Organization Type and Purpose

The Defense Budget Project of the Center on Budget and Policy is committed to a coherent U.S. national security policy that reflects a realistic assessment of available fiscal resources and national defense needs.

Internships

One internship is offered each semester and during the summer to a highly motivated undergraduate interested in defense policy economics or political science. The position is designed to reflect an intern's particular interest in conjunction with the project's needs. Interns assist staff with legislative issues, conduct research, and prepare material for the press.

Qualifications

Applicants should have research, fact-finding, and writing skills and be willing to carry out administrative as well as substantive tasks.

Internship Dates and Duration

Internships are available year-round and usually last for three months.

Funding/Academic Credit

Full-time interns receive $150 per week. The project will work with students to arrange school credit.

To Apply

Two to three months prior to the anticipated start of the internship, an applicant should send a resume, letter of interest, and small writing sample, along with the names and phone numbers of three references.

Women at the Defense Budget Project

Of the staff, 50 percent are women; 40 percent of interns are women.

Contact Person

Carol Lessure, Outreach and Intern Coordinator; Defense Budget Project, 236 Massachusetts Avenue NE, Suite 301, Washington, DC 20002; (202) 546-9737.

East-West Center

1777 East-West Road
Honolulu, HI 96848
(808) 944-7111

Organization Type and Purpose

The center was founded by Congress in 1960 to promote better relations between the United States and the nations of Asia and the Pacific through cooperative study, training, and research. The center's 220 professional staff are all based in Honolulu.

Internships

Internships are available to undergraduate and graduate student researchers and potential U.S. and Asian leaders. Interns pursue research on topics of concern to the center.

Qualifications

Interns should be working toward an undergraduate or graduate degree.

Internship Dates and Duration

Internships can last from several months to a year.

Funding/Academic Credit

Positions are funded.

To Apply

Contact the office of student affairs and open grants at the address below. Indicate area of interest among the following: Institute of Culture and Communication, Environment and Policy Institute, Population Institute, Resource Systems Institute, and the Pacific Islands Development Program.

Women at the Center

No information available.

Contact Person

Awards Service Officer; East-West Center, 1777 East-West Road, Honolulu, HI 96848; (808) 944-7111.

Ford Foundation

320 East 43rd Street
New York, NY 10017
(212) 573-5000

Organization Type and Purpose

The Ford Foundation is a private philanthropic organization that grants funds for activities in areas of urban and rural poverty resources, human rights, government, education, culture, international affairs, and population issues.

Internships

Paid summer internships are offered in New Delhi, India; Lima, Peru; and Mexico City, Mexico. Interns assist program officers in reviewing funding requests, preparing program reports, and evaluating completed reports. Internships available in the United States focus on projects on rural and urban poverty, international affairs, and human rights.

Qualifications

Applicants should be graduate students in the social sciences, particularly in area studies, international affairs, political science, or related fields. Candidates should have analytical and conceptual skills and be good writers. Fluency in Spanish is required for the Lima and Mexico City programs.

Internship Dates and Duration

A summer program is available.

Funding/Academic Credit

A monthly stipend of $1,000 – $2,000 is provided.

To Apply

Applicants should submit a resume, a writing sample, a brief statement of career aims, and three references.

Women at the Ford Foundation

Of the entire Ford Foundation staff, 68 percent are women. Although the percentage of women interns varies, it has been approximately 50 percent in recent years.

Contact Person

Jane Russin, Assistant Manager of Employment and Training Personnel; Ford Foundation, 320 East 43rd Street, New York, NY 10017; (212) 573-5000.

Foreign Policy Association

729 Seventh Avenue
New York, NY 10019
(212) 764-4050

Organization Type and Purpose

The Foreign Policy Association is a national, nonpartisan organization dedicated to educating American citizens on foreign policy. A nonprofit network, the association publishes the annual *Great Decisions* study and discussion guide, along with the bimonthly *Headline Series* and special reports on timely topics.

Internships

Undergraduates and graduates may apply for unpaid internships offered during the summer and academic year. Interns usually work in the editorial or public affairs departments, where they assist editorial staff in research or writing and help the public affairs staff in marketing materials.

Qualifications

Qualifications vary according to the assignment. The editorial department generally seeks interns with a background in history and international affairs and with strong writing skills.

Internship Dates and Duration

Positions are available during the summer and academic year. Interns may also work during a one-month winter term.

Funding/Academic Credit

Positions are unpaid; credit is not available.

To Apply

Contact either Thetis Reavis or Nancy Hoepli, editor in chief, for further information.

Women at FPA

Of the staff, 83 percent are women (25 out of 30); women usually comprise slightly more than half of the interns.

Contact Person

Thetis Reavis, Vice President of Public Affairs; Foreign Policy Association, 729 Seventh Avenue, New York, NY 10019; (212) 764-4050.

Free University—Washington, Paris, Moscow

4301 Connecticut Avenue NW
Washington, DC 20008
(202) 364-0200

Organization Type and Purpose

The primary purpose of the nonprofit Free University is to provide Soviet and Eastern European students with access to American and Western European universities through correspondence courses. Workshops, seminars, and conferences on East-West affairs are also offered. The summer school is the Free University's primary focus at this time.

Internships

Interns act as liaisons between the Soviet and Eastern European students and their professors, selecting, purchasing, and mailing educational and other material. They also write articles on Soviet affairs and plan and organize an international summer program on U.S.-Soviet affairs for graduate students.

Qualifications

A strong interest in international affairs and Russian studies is desired. Russian language ability preferred but is not required.

Internship Dates and Duration

Not specified.

Funding/Academic Credit

Positions are not funded.

To Apply

Apply by letter or phone call.

Women at the Free University

Approximately 50 percent of the staff and interns are women.

Contact Person

Edward Lozansky, Executive Director; Free University, 4301 Connecticut Avenue NW, Washington, DC 20008; (202) 364-0200.

Friends Committee on National Legislation

245 Second Street NE
Washington, DC 20002
(202) 547-6000

Organization Type and Purpose

The Friends Committee is an active expression of the concern of the Religious Society of Friends for the shaping of U.S. public policy. Priorities include opposing military aid and arms exports and supporting worldwide disarmament.

Internships

This is an opportunity for young persons to invest a year assisting the legislative staff in the committee's ongoing program. Interns are assigned to organization lobbyists to provide backup support for various legislative programs. Interns are considered full-time staff members for the duration of appointment. The committee strives to provide a meaningful and satisfying work assignment consonant with the needs of the legislative program.

Qualifications

Candidates are chosen based on educational backgrounds, related work and volunteer experience, past association with Society of Friends' activities, commitment to the committee's work, and the evaluation of references.

Internship Dates and Duration

Paid internships require an 11-month commitment starting in September; unpaid positions are for 3 to 6 months each quarter.

Funding/Academic Credit

Funded positions include a stipend of about $800 per month, with basic medical coverage provided.

To Apply

Apply March 15 for paid, year-long positions; quarterly interns should apply two to three months in advance. Contact the committee for application form.

Women at the Committee

No information available.

Contact Person

Michael Brauner, Director of Administration; Friends Committee on National Legislation, 245 Second Street NE, Washington, DC 20002; (202) 547-6000.

Heritage Foundation

214 Massachusetts Avenue NE
Washington, DC 20002
(202) 546-4400

Organization Type and Purpose

The Heritage Foundation is a nonprofit research organization with a public policy agenda based on a free-market economy, limited government, and strong national defense. The foundation's publications include the *Policy Review* and the *Critical Issues* monograph series. The Heritage Resource Bank comprises 1,000 scholars and 450 research groups, all of whom assist the foundation in reaching out to Washington movers and shakers.

Internships

Undergraduate and graduate students may participate in semester or summer internships in Heritage's research department. Work involves basic fact gathering, library research, and clerical duties.

Qualifications

Candidates should demonstrate a commitment to conservative goals as well as an interest in world affairs.

Internship Dates and Duration

Fifteen to 20 interns are selected each summer from some 100-150 applicants. A smaller number of interns is selected during the academic year.

Funding/Academic Credit

Summer positions are funded at $175 per week; internships at other times are unpaid.

To Apply

Submit a resume with a cover letter explaining interests. Applicants should also provide references or letters of recommendation, along with any other pertinent materials, such as a short writing sample. The deadline for summer is March 15 (although applications can be taken as early as January). Other terms have flexible deadlines.

Women at Heritage

Approximately 30 percent of the total staff are women.

Contact Person

Robert Huberty, Director of the Resource Bank; Heritage Foundation, 214 Massachusetts Avenue NE, Washington, DC 20002; (202) 546-4400.

Institute for Foreign Policy Analysis

675 Massachusetts Avenue
10th floor
Cambridge, MA 02139-3396
(617) 492-2116

Washington Office:
1612 K Street NW
Suite 1204
Washington, DC 20006
(202) 463-7942

Organization Type and Purpose

The institute undertakes research, convenes conferences and seminars, publishes studies, and engages in programs to strengthen education in foreign policy and national security affairs.

Internships

Interns, who are known as research assistants, undertake basic research on regular institute projects. They assist senior- and intermediate-level staff in preparing reports and other material. The institute normally has two or three staff research assistants to familiarize promising students with policy analysis and the benefits of interdisciplinary teamwork and to introduce them to the political and strategic aspects of foreign policy.

Qualifications

Candidates must possess an undergraduate degree in international relations, political science, modern history, and/or related subjects. IFPA, however, prefers interns who possess a master's degree in these areas or at least are enrolled in a graduate degree program.

Internship Dates and Duration

Typical internships begin in June. They are full time in the summer. Part-time, year-round internships begin when specific positions open.

Funding/Academic Credit

Interns are generally paid on an hourly basis; no educational credits are given.

To Apply

Write a letter, enclosing a resume, references, and a 20- to 30-page writing sample.

Women at the Institute

Of the staff, 37 percent are women.

Contact Person

Robert C. Herber, Treasurer; Institute for Foreign Policy Analysis, 1612 K Street NW, Suite 1204, Washington, DC 20006, (202) 463-7942; in Cambridge, call (617) 492-2116.

Institute for International Economics

11 Dupont Circle NW
Washington, DC 20036
(202) 328-0583

Organization Type and Purpose

The organization focuses on policy issues, including the relationship of international economic and security issues.

Internships

Interns work as research assistants with senior staff, organizing meetings and conferences. In general, internships include some clerical duties.

Qualifications

Significant training in economics is preferred.

Internship Dates and Duration

Positions are available on a summer or semester basis.

Funding/Academic Credit

Funding of $7.00 per hour is provided; no other benefits.

To Apply

The deadline for summer is in February. Apply for semester internship six months in advance. Send a letter and resume to the institute.

Women at IIE

Of the permanent research assistants, 15 percent to 20 percent are women, while 50 percent of the interns are women. The institute encourages qualified women and minorities to apply.

Contact Person

Tom Bayard, Deputy Director; Institute for International Economics, 11 Dupont Circle NW, Washington, DC 20036; (202) 328-0583.

Institute for Policy Studies

1601 Connecticut Avenue NW
Washington, DC 20009
(202) 234-9382

Organization Type and Purpose

IPS, a center for research, education, and social intervention, focuses on national security, foreign policy, international economics, human rights, and domestic issues. The institute holds conferences; publishes books, papers, and a journal; and sponsors the Washington School. IPS' sister organization, the Transnational Institute, is based in Amsterdam, with a staff of European scholars and activists.

Internships

Both semester and summer unpaid internships are open to college students who have an interest and some experience in either domestic or foreign policy. Responsibilities include research, independent study, and administrative assistance.

Internship Dates and Duration

Summer and semester-length internships are available.

Funding/Academic Credit

Internships are unpaid.

To Apply

Contact the internship coordinator.

Women at the Institute

No information available.

Contact Person

Lesley Rose, Internship Coordinator; Institute for Policy Studies, 1601 Connecticut Avenue NW, Washington, DC 20009; (202) 234-9382.

Institute for Soviet-American Relations

1608 New Hampshire Avenue NW
Washington, DC 20009
(202) 387-3034

Organization Type and Purpose

This is a small, nonprofit, nonpartisan organization that works to improve U.S.-Soviet relations. ISAR attempts to make connections between people, ideas, and systems, and to better relations between the two countries. The group publishes a handbook on organizations involved in U.S.-Soviet relations, another on U.S.-Soviet space bridges (satellite communications), a manual for exchanges, and a journal that collects and disseminates information about developments in U.S.-Soviet relations.

Internships

Interns work on the institute journal, gathering information, researching articles and checking facts, and assisting in layout and composition. They also respond to mail queries, answer telephones, and perform other administrative duties. Interns have the opportunity to attend events related to U.S.-Soviet activities.

Qualifications

Interns should have an interest in journal production. General office experience and attention to detail are helpful.

Internship Dates and Duration

Summer opportunities and school-year internships available.

Funding/Academic Credit

Positions are funded at $100 per month.

To Apply

Send resume and cover letter to the contact person.

Women at ISAR

Staff is currently composed entirely of women.

Contact Person

Tatiana Bachuretz, Editorial Assistant; Institute for Soviet-American Relations, 1608 New Hampshire Avenue NW, Washington, DC 20009; (202) 387-3034.

International Center for Development Policy

731 Eighth Street SE
Washington, DC 20003
(202) 547-3800

Organization Type and Purpose

The International Center is a foreign policy organization focused on relating with countries in Asia, Africa, and Latin America. This nonprofit, advocacy, and research center seeks to inform the press, Congress, and government officials of the impact of U.S. policies abroad.

Internships

Four to six interns work with the center each semester. Interns are involved in every facet of its work: conducting investigative research, helping organize delegations, and monitoring legislative developments. The first few weeks of an internship are spent becoming familiar with each of the five commissions which together comprise the center. Since the center is small, interns are allowed to get involved in all aspects of the organization.

Qualifications

Candidates should be college juniors or above. Language skills are helpful but not required.

Internship Dates and Duration

Internships last about 10 weeks to four months at various times during the year. In fall, from September to December; in winter, from January to April; and in summer, from May to August.

Funding/Academic Credit

No information available.

To Apply

Send a resume and short writing sample with a cover letter containing available dates. Recommendations are not required. Deadlines: fall, August 1; winter, December 1; summer, April 1.

Women at the Center

The staff is composed of 50 percent women.

Contact Person

Wardell Sanders, Internship Coordinator; International Center for Development Policy, 731 Eighth Street SE, Washington, DC 20003; (202) 547-3800.

Kennan Institute for Advanced Russian Studies

Wilson Center, Smithsonian Institution
955 L'Enfant Plaza, Suite 7400
Washington, DC 20560
(202) 287-3105

Organization Type and Purpose

The Kennan Institute is housed in the Woodrow Wilson International Center for Scholars. Fellows of the center engage in research, prepare publications, and organize seminars and dialogues with outside scholars and public/private officials. The institute supports research on a wide range of topics relating to the Soviet Union. With access to the finest libraries for Russian-Soviet studies in the West, the institute is a kind of Washington embassy for students of Soviet affairs.

Internships

Candidates assist Kennan fellows or research scholars. Interns become involved in the international atmosphere of an institution dedicated to the highest scholarly pursuits. They can attend special events sponsored by the center, including discussions, colloquiums, and seminars.

Qualifications

Undergraduate juniors and seniors, graduate students, and recent graduates may apply. Applicants should have a good command of Russian.

Internship Dates and Duration

Internships are offered in the fall, spring, and summer. Some 15-20 hours per week are expected.

Funding/Academic Credit

Depending on hours worked, the stipend is approximately $210 to $280 per month. Work-study funds are available for eligible students.

To Apply

Applicants should send a detailed resume, two letters of recommendation from faculty members, and an academic transcript.

Women at the Kennan Institute

No information available.

Contact Person

Theodore Taranovski, Research Associate; Kennan Institute for Advanced Russian Studies, Wilson Center, Smithsonian Institution, 955 L'Enfant Plaza, Suite 7400, Washington, DC 20560; (202) 287-3105.

Middle East Institute

1761 N Street NW
Washington, DC 20036
(202) 785-1141

Organization Type and Purpose

The nonprofit Middle East Institute strives to foster American understanding of the Middle East through lectures, conferences, panels, educational courses, publications, a library and research center, and the Islamic Affairs program. The institute refrains from taking any institutional position on the many controversies endemic to the Middle East; by charter and tradition, it may neither become the instrument of anyone's policy nor seek to influence legislation.

Internships

Interns assist the program department or work on the *Middle East Journal.*

Qualifications

No information available.

Internship Dates and Duration

Positions offered during school semesters and in the summer.

Funding/Academic Credit

No funding is available, but credit can be arranged.

To Apply

Interviews are required; submit a resume with cover letter.

Women at the Institute

Of the staff, 75 percent are women, as are 75 percent of interns.

Contact Person

Betsy Chapin, Program Assistant; Middle East Institute, 1761 N Street NW, Washington, DC 20036; (202) 785-1141.

National Campaign to Save the ABM Treaty

1601 Connecticut Avenue NW
Suite 704
Washington, DC 20009
(202) 939-5770

Organization Type and Purpose

The campaign is a nonpartisan coalition of prominent national organizations and distinguished individuals dedicated to preserving and strengthening the 1972 Anti-Ballistic Missile Treaty, which is the cornerstone of efforts to reduce the nuclear arms race. The campaign's report entitled "The Impact of U.S. and Soviet Ballistic Missile Defense Programs on the ABM Treaty" is the only comprehensive treatment of the subject available to the general public. The campaign also publishes a 120-page briefing book on the ABM Treaty and related issues.

Internships

Interns are involved in virtually all aspects of the organization's work due in part to its small staff. Responsibilities include monitoring legislative hearings, coordinating activities with like-minded groups, preparing editorials for newspapers, responding to inquiries, researching and writing campaign materials, and carrying out administrative tasks.

Qualifications

Internships are open to undergraduates and graduates who are energetic and personable and have a strong interest in, familiarity with, and commitment to arms control issues.

Internship Dates and Duration

Positions are offered for 10-12 weeks year-round.

Funding/Academic Credit

Internships are not funded but the campaign can help arrange academic credit. Local transportation costs to and from work can be reimbursed.

To Apply

Deadlines are flexible. Send a writing sample, resume, and letters of recommendation to the contact below.

Women at the Campaign

Women comprise 50 percent of staff and interns.

Contact Person

Bill Monahan, Campaign Coordinator; National Campaign to Save the ABM Treaty, 1601 Connecticut Avenue NW, Suite 704, Washington, DC 20009; (202) 939-5770.

National Defense Foundation

225 North Washington Street
Alexandria, VA 22314
(703) 549-0311

Organization Type and Purpose

The National Defense Foundation (of the Non-Commissioned Officers Association) focuses on defense manpower issues and assists the Department of Defense with its nonpartisan voter registration and education campaign. The nonprofit group also endeavors to educate Congress on the need for a strong armed service.

Internships

Interns assist staff in the Pentagon office. They research, write, and edit reports on such topics as the military retirement structure, retention, total force structure policies, pay compensation, absentee voting, and military family problems.

Qualifications

Primary skills include writing, researching, editing, and the ability to type. An understanding of and interest in defense issues is important.

Internship Dates and Duration

The internship period runs 15 weeks during semesters.

Funding/Academic Credit

A stipend of $20 per week is available.

To Apply

Contact the Washington Center (see "Special Internship Programs"), or the contact listed below for more information.

Women at National Defense Foundation

No information available.

Contact Person

Tom Ryan, Executive Director; National Defense Foundation, 225 North Washington Street, Alexandria, VA 22314; (703) 549-0311.

National Security Agency

M321
Fort Meade, MD 20755-6000
(301) 859-6161

Organization Type and Purpose

Established in 1952, the NSA is the federal agency responsible for U.S. communications, security activities, the production of foreign intelligence information, and computer security. Its highly classified work involves the development and operation of extensive cryptographic systems.

Internships

NSA participates in the Cooperative Education Program (Co-op) and the Summer Employment Program (see "Special Internship Programs"). The former program is full time; the latter, summer only. Co-op students participate in rotating assignments related to their academic discipline and interests.

Qualifications

NSA seeks Co-op students majoring in Middle Eastern, Asian, Slavic, and other East European languages. For the summer program, responsibilities and qualifications are similar to those of Co-op positions. Applicants must be U.S. citizens and have a 3.0 or better GPA.

Internship Dates and Duration

Students work on translation, transcription, reportage, and analysis. Summer participants work the summer following their junior year.

Funding/Academic Credit

Positions are paid.

To Apply

Applicants should contact the agency at least six months before graduation. Students should check with their college placement office to arrange for an interview with a visiting NSA representative. Interested persons should also contact the agency.

Women at NSA

No information available.

Contact Person

Bill Nix, Placement Officer; National Security Agency, M321, Fort Meade, MD 20755-6000; (301) 859-6161.

National Security Archive

1755 Massachusetts Avenue NW, Suite 500
Washington, DC 20036
(202) 797-0882

Organization Type and Purpose

The archive provides scholars and researchers with documentation on a variety of foreign policy issues collected from primary source material, including declassified government documents.

Internships

Interns work with project teams assigned to a specific foreign policy or national security topic. An effort is made to accommodate the intern's area of interest. Work includes building chronologies, analyzing and indexing government documents, entering computer data, performing library research, attending hearings, and helping with some office tasks.

Qualifications

The archive prefers junior and senior college students but will accept sophomores. An interest in international politics, area or government studies, or national security issues is helpful.

Internship Dates and Duration

A two-month commitment is preferred; interns are accepted year-round.

Funding/Academic Credit

The internship is unpaid, although funding may become available for travel to and from work. Academic credit can be arranged. The deadlines are somewhat flexible, but in general they are August 1 for fall, December 1 for spring, and April 1 for summer.

To Apply

Students are encouraged to apply as early as possible. Submit a resume and transcript, a short writing sample, and two letters of recommendation from professors. Indicate in a cover letter areas of interest, time constraints, and a telephone number. Interviews will be held by phone or in person.

Women at the Archive

The organization is particularly interested in opportunities for women and minorities. Women presently constitute about 20 percent of the staff; the percentage of women interns varies over time.

Contact Person

Nicole Ball, Director of Analysis; National Security Archive, 1755 Massachusetts Avenue NW, Suite 500, Washington, DC 20036; (202) 797-0882.

Nicaragua Network

2025 I Street NW
Suite 212
Washington, DC 20006
(202) 223-2328

Organization Type and Purpose

This nonprofit group is comprised of more than 250 local committees working to promote peace and understanding between the United States and Nicaragua.

Internships

Interns work on four of the network's main activities: mobilizing local individuals to lobby against *contra* aid; organizing work brigades to help build houses and schools in Nicaragua; raising funds for humanitarian aid directed at the Nicaraguan people; and running an information office, which produces a bimonthly newsletter. Internships involve a fair amount of routine office work. However, the staff is friendly and upbeat, and incoming mail includes an enormous volume of current information about Central America, which interns are encouraged to read.

Qualifications

A commitment to the goals of the network is desired. Good verbal and written communication skills are necessary.

Internship Dates and Duration

Work schedule is flexible.

Funding/Academic Credit

A stipend is provided for transportation within Washington, DC.

To Apply

Write or call the network for an application.

Women at the Network

Of the staff, 60 percent are women; women comprise 50 percent of interns.

Contact Person

Pat Clark, Intern Coordinator; Nicaragua Network, 2025 I Street NW, Suite 212, Washington, DC 20006; (202) 223-2328.

Office for Church in Society

104 Madison Avenue
New York, NY 10016
(212) 683-5656

Washington Office:
110 Maryland Avenue NE, Suite 504
Washington, DC 20002
(202) 543-1517

Organization Type and Purpose

The OCS is one of 10 national agencies of the United Church of Christ; it is responsible for coordinating the denomination's work on social issues, advocating denominational policy, and developing programs of education and action on these issues.

Internships

Responsibilities include working with a staff of 10, with responsibility for servicing and mobilizing the UCC public policy, peace, and justice network. The primary task is contacting the network leadership around the country by phone to keep them up-to-date on issues before Congress. UCC has a commitment to affirmative action and seeks qualified women and minority candidates.

Qualifications

Internships are available each year to those seeking a position in which to gain experience in national organizing within the religious community.

Internship Dates and Duration

The Washington office offers year-long internships, usually beginning around July 1.

Funding/Academic Credit

A stipend of $10,500 a year is generally offered although the amount may vary from year to year. Deadline for a term beginning July 1 is May 1.

To Apply

Send a resume with three references, including phone numbers; a one-page letter indicating why position is sought; and religious affiliation and interest. Also enclose college or seminary transcript, and note any computer and organizing experience.

Women at the Office for Church in Society

Of the 20 staff members, 14 are women.

Contact Person

Jay Litner, Office Director; Office for Church in Society, 110 Maryland Ave. NE, Suite 504, Washington, DC 20002; (202) 543-1517; in New York City, call (212) 683-5656.

Organization for American-Soviet Exchanges

1302 R Street NW
Washington, DC 20009
(202) 332-1145

Organization Type and Purpose

OASES is a nongovernmental, nonprofit organization that promotes unofficial professional, educational, and cultural exchanges on a mutual basis between the peoples of the United States and the Soviet Union.

Internships

Interns' duties generally fall into one of three areas: fund-raising, hosting projects, or working in the Interpreting Services Division. Aside from one of these areas, interns also work closely with the executive director, answering inquiries about OASES.

Qualifications

An interest in our organization is the only qualification. Students who speak Russian will have the opportunity to translate and interpret.

Internship Dates and Duration

No information available.

Funding/Academic Credit

No information available.

To Apply

Contact the organization at the address below. Internships are usually filled through the Washington Center.

Women at OASES

No information available.

Contact Person

Intern Coordinator; Organization for American-Soviet Exchanges, 1302 R Street NW, Washington, DC 20009; (202) 332-1145.

Physicians for Social Responsibility

1601 Connecticut Avenue NW
Suite 800
Washington, DC 20009
(202) 785-3777

Organization Type and Purpose

Founded in 1961, PSR is an organization of some 70,000 doctors and supporters who work to educate the public about the medical perils of both nuclear weapons and nuclear war. It is affiliated with the Nobel Peace Prize-winning International Physicians for the Prevention of Nuclear War. PSR has a national office in Washington and 157 chapters across the country.

Internships

Positions are available in the Program Department, which oversees chapter development and implements educational programs, including symposia, the annual meeting, and the Soviet-American Physicians Campaign. The policy, legislation, and communications offices also accept interns depending on need. Interns assume various tasks, from writing briefing papers and handbooks to attending arms control strategy sessions on Capitol Hill and helping with mailings.

Qualifications

Qualifications depend on positions available.

Internship Dates and Duration

Summer, spring, winter, and fall internships are available based on PSR requirements.

Funding/Academic Credit

A $100-a-week stipend is available.

To Apply

Send a resume, writing sample, two letters of reference, dates of availability for an interview in Washington, and length of desired internship to the contact below.

Women at PSR

No information available.

Contact Person

Jennifer Vasiloff, Administrative Assistant; Physicians for Social Responsibility, 1601 Connecticut Avenue NW, Suite 800, Washington, DC 20009; (202) 785-3777.

Professionals' Coalition for Nuclear Arms Control

1616 P Street NW
Suite 320
Washington, DC 20036
(202) 332-4823

Organization Type and Purpose

This nonprofit group is a lobbying coalition of professionals committed to stopping the nuclear arms race. It works to coordinate and direct professionals' expertise and commitment into organized and effective legislative action.

Internships

Interns assist in identifying and organizing coalition members into activist teams in key states and congressional districts, alerting members to upcoming arms control votes, coordinating strategies to influence their senators and representatives, tracking arms control legislation, and attending relevant congressional debates and hearings.

Qualifications

Applicants should have an interest in arms control issues, excellent communication skills, and the ability to work with a diverse membership of professionals.

Internship Dates and Duration

Positions require working four to five days a week for a minimum of three months.

Funding/Academic Credit

Interns may receive academic credit; local travel expenses are reimbursed.

To Apply

Deadlines are flexible. Send a resume, a cover letter specifying interest in the position, and references.

Women at the Coalition

Of the staff, 25 percent are women. In recent years all interns have been women.

Contact Person

Robert Musil, Executive Director; Professionals' Coalition for Nuclear Arms Control, 1616 P Street NW, Suite 320, Washington, DC 20036; (202) 332-4823.

RAND Corporation

1700 Main Street
P.O. Box 2138
Santa Monica, CA 90406-2138
(213) 393-0411

Organization Type and Purpose

RAND is a center for research and analysis on national security and public welfare issues. A resident staff of some 550 research professionals is augmented by about 400 consultants, covering many disciplines.

Internships

About 20 students participate in the program each year. They do research that can be completed usually within three months, often on a topic related to their dissertation. The program's objectives are to introduce outstanding graduate students to RAND and to produce and publish research using RAND's techniques of interdisciplinary policy analysis.

Qualifications

Students should have completed at least one year of graduate study toward their Ph.D. Although most RAND work does not require a security clearance, possessing one allows students more freedom within the facilities and fosters interaction among the staff.

Internship Dates and Duration

Most students are in residence during the summer months although other times can be arranged.

Funding/Academic Credit

Salaries for participants are competitive in the summer-work marketplace. RAND pays travel expenses to and from the workplace.

To Apply

Submit applications early in the calendar year. Interested graduate students should send a resume and cover letter to the contact below. To allow time for clearance procedures, participants are usually chosen by late April. RAND is an affirmative action employer and welcomes applications from qualified women, minority, and disabled students.

Women at RAND

No information available.

Contact Person

Kenneth Logan, Personnel Officer; RAND Corporation, 1700 Main Street, P.O. Box 2138, Santa Monica, CA 90406-2138; (213) 393-0411.

Student Pugwash USA

1638 R Street NW
Washington, DC 20009
(202) 328-6555

Organization Type and Purpose

Student Pugwash USA is a nonprofit educational organization run by students and young professionals.

Internships

Student Pugwash provides university students with a range of programs to prepare them as future leaders and concerned citizens better able to make thoughtful decisions about the use of technology. Interns work as staff members, taking part in office discussions and decisions. Programs include working with students to promote campus discussion of the ethical dimensions of science and technology; working on the biennial conference in which students and senior participants conduct a week-long forum; or working on publications.

Qualifications

Individual initiative and responsibility are encouraged. All academic backgrounds are appropriate. Scientific and technological backgrounds are not required, but an interest in these fields is needed. Good communication skills and sharp writing abilities are important, as is flexibility.

Internship Dates and Duration

Periods of internship are flexible.

Funding/Academic Credit

A small stipend may be available; academic credit can be arranged.

To Apply

Contact the office.

Women at Student Pugwash

Approximately 66 percent of the staff are women.

Contact Person

Ellen Crowe, Executive Assistant; Student Pugwash USA, 1638 R Street NW, Washington, DC 20009; (202) 328-6555.

Union of Concerned Scientists

1616 P Street NW
Suite 310
Washington, DC 20036
(202) 332-0900

Organization Type and Purpose

UCS is a national organization of more than 100,000 scientists and citizens concerned about the impact of advanced technology on society. The group currently focuses on the issues of nuclear energy and nuclear arms, specifically on how to control the arms race and ways to promote a safe energy policy.

Internships

Interns work in the media program, on research, and on organizing grass-roots lobbying of members of Congress.

Qualifications

Applicants should be committed to the goals of UCS, have strong oral and written communication skills, be self-motivated, and able to work independently. The media internship requires some clerical work, a familiarity with computers, and an interest in how the press operates and covers arms control and nuclear energy issues.

Internship Dates and Duration

Internships require 40 hours per week and cover a minimum of three months.

Funding/Academic Credit

Interns receive a stipend of $500 a month and may also receive academic credit.

To Apply

Applications are accepted year-round. Deadlines: for winter, November 1; for summer, April 1; for fall, July 1. Send a resume, a completed application form (call UCS for a copy), the phone numbers of two references, and a writing sample to the contact below.

Women at UCS

No information available.

Contact Person

Rosemary Frazel, Internship Coordinator; Union of Concerned Scientists, 1616 P Street NW, Suite 310, Washington, DC 20036; (202) 332-0900.

United Campuses to Prevent Nuclear War

309 Pennsylvania Avenue SE
Washington, DC 20003
(202) 675-4354

Organization Type and Purpose

UCAM's mission is to halt the nuclear arms race and foster world peace through a campus-based movement involving university students, faculty, and staff. The organization monitors activities in Congress and, with other peace groups, works to influence the course of legislation.

Internships

During the spring semester, two to three interns participate in preparing for UCAM's annual spring event: Lobby Day in Washington. Interns also assist with public information—communicating with chapters and members throughout the country, writing newsletter articles, researching issues, and monitoring congressional hearings.

Qualifications

A strong interest in peace education, conflict resolution, and related fields is necessary. For some assignments, special skills may be important: an intern who has prior experience in putting out newsletters or other publications, along with strong writing skills, might be especially valuable.

Internship Dates and Duration

Internships are available for summer, fall, and winter semester periods.

Funding/Academic Credit

Budget permitting, small stipends can be arranged. UCAM will also help interns with credit arrangements.

To Apply

Applications are accepted year-round. A personal interview is preferred. Students interested initially work through their institutions or through such programs as American University's Washington Semester or the Washington Center. Otherwise, queries can be made directly to UCAM. Send a resume to contact below.

Women at UCAM

Current staff includes three full-time employees: two women, one man; a volunteer with the International Christian Youth Exchange (woman); and three student interns (one woman, two men).

Contact Person

Vivian H. Mills, Executive Director; United Campuses to Prevent Nuclear War, 309 Pennsylvania Avenue SE, Washington, DC 20003; (202) 675-4354.

United Nations

S-2429
Office of Personnel
New York, NY 10017
(212) 963-4437

Organization Type and Purpose

The UN is an international organization created to coordinate global political activity and to promote world peace.

Internships

The United Nations offers a number of opportunities: a position with the Department of Public Information; the graduate student program; the ad hoc internship program; a position with the UN Institute for Training and Research (UNITAR); and the UN Development summer program. Several specialized agencies also have internships. Each internship opportunity is different. Some are located at the UN headquarters in New York, others are in Geneva.

Qualifications

Most internship programs are geared toward graduate students and visiting scholars; however, exceptional undergraduates are sometimes accepted for the ad hoc program.

Internship Dates and Duration

Most positions are for the summer, except for the ad hoc and UNITAR programs. Deadlines and application procedures vary according to the program. The ad hoc internship is best suited to undergraduates; it is offered in the spring, summer, and fall semesters for a minimum period of two months.

Funding/Academic Credit

Internships are not funded. Travel costs and other arrangements are the responsibility of interns.

To Apply

Contact intern coordinator for specifics of each program.

Women at the U.N.

No information available.

Contact Person

Ann Hubbard, Intern Coordinator; United Nations, S-2429, Office of Personnel, New York, NY 10017; (212) 963-4437.

United Nations Association of the U.S.A.

485 Fifth Avenue
New York, NY 10017
(212) 697-3232

Washington Office:
1010 Vermont Avenue NW
Washington, DC 20005
(202) 347-5004

Organization Type and Purpose

UNA-USA is a national, nonprofit organization that conducts programs of research, study, and information to heighten public awareness and knowledge of global issues and their relationship to the United Nations. The organization comprises a network of 165 chapters and 130 affiliated national organizations. UNA-USA coordinates a national UN Day program, analyzes current international economic problems through its Economic Policy Council, and works with business executives through its Corporate Council for International Policy.

Internships

Internships involve research on international issues and often include attendance at various UN meetings and UNA functions.

Qualifications

Candidates should have good research, writing, and English grammar skills. A strong international affairs background is also important.

Internship Dates and Duration

Internships are available all year.

Funding/Academic Credit

Positions are not funded.

To Apply

Contact the national program director for an application form. Deadlines: for summer, April 1; for fall, August 19; for spring, January 15 (all dates approximate).

Women at the Organization

Of the staff, 68 percent are women. The number of women interns varies with projects and time of year.

Contact Person

Carol Christian, Director of Field Administration; United Nations Association of the U.S.A., 485 Fifth Avenue, New York, NY 10017; (212) 697-3232; in Washington, call (202) 347-5004.

U.S. Army Judge Advocate General's Corps

Professional Recruiting Office
Fort Belvoir, VA 22060-5818
(202) 664-6416 or 1-800-336-3315

Organization Type and Purpose

The JAGC is a military organization.

Internships

The JAG Corps hires 100 law students each summer to work in Army legal offices throughout the United States and West Germany. Interns are supervised by an attorney and perform legal research, write briefs and opinions, conduct investigations, interview witnesses, and otherwise assist in preparing civil or criminal cases. Duties include reviewing government contracts, investigating and adjudicating claims for and against the United States based on tort liability, and trying criminal cases.

Qualifications

Law students should have proven scholastic ability and have demonstrated leadership potential. Applicants must be U.S. citizens and full-time students at a law school; those in four-year programs are eligible after completion of their second year of law school.

Internship Dates and Duration

Internships cover a 90-day period during the summer.

Funding/Academic Credit

Funding for first-year students is on a GS-5 pay scale, and for second-year students on a GS-7 pay scale.

To Apply

First-year students should apply by March 7, second-year students by November 7. Submit forms (DAJA-PT Form 13 and Standard Form 171), resume, and undergraduate and law school transcripts to Army JAGC Professional Recruiting Office (summer intern), Building 1834, Franklin Road, Fort Belvoir, VA 22060-5818. A personal interview must be arranged prior to the application deadline date. The JAG Corps actively seeks applications from women and minority-group members. For more information, call toll free 1-800-336-3315 or in Virginia (703) 664-6416.

Women at JAGC

No information available.

Contact Person

Capt. Jon J. Canerday, Recruiting Officer; U.S. Army Judge Advocate General's Corps, Professional Recruiting Office, Fort Belvoir, VA 22060-5818; (202) 664-6416.

U.S.-Asia Institute

232 East Capitol Street NE
Washington, DC 20003
(202) 544-3181

Organization Type and Purpose

This nonprofit, nonpartisan organization is dedicated to fostering and strengthening ties between the people and governments of the United States and Asia. Through research symposia and publications, it examines the relevant economic, political, security, and cultural issues. The institute sponsors an annual conference, congressional tours to Asia, and a quarterly newsletter.

Internships

The institute staff is small, and students are given a fair amount of responsibility. Two to three undergraduate and/or graduate students are selected to work in the Washington office as staff assistants. Interns are given responsibilities normally associated with full-time professional staff, such as tracking legislation, writing research, compiling the newsletter, preparing for the annual conference, and representing the institute. The internship program offers the student an opportunity to learn about U.S.-Asia relations while gaining insight into the U.S. policy-making process.

Qualifications

Qualifications include maturity, excellent writing and oral skills, and a combination of research, analytical, and logistical abilities.

Internship Dates and Duration

Internships are flexible, structured around academic terms. Hours vary from 16 to 40 hours a week.

Funding/Academic Credit

Through two memorial funds, two internships are funded in the summer: one is for $1,000; the other for $2,000. Academic credit can be arranged through the candidate's college.

To Apply

Deadlines: for spring, December 10; for summer, April 15; for winter, August 10. Send a resume with a brief writing sample to the contact below.

Women at the Institute

Currently, 66 percent of the staff and 75 percent of interns are women.

Contact Person

Mary Sue Bissell, Executive Director; U.S.-Asia Institute, 232 East Capitol Street NE, Washington, DC 20003; (202) 544-3181.

U.S. Department of Defense

Pentagon
Washington, DC 20301
(202) 697-7173

Organization Type and Purpose

The Defense Department is responsible for providing the military forces needed to deter war and protect the security of the United States. The major elements of these forces are the Army, Navy, Air Force, and Marine Corps. The department also includes a significant number of civilian employees who work on issues ranging from arms control and strategic policy to the technical aspects of weapons development and procurement.

Internships

The Civil Service Reform Act of 1978 enabled federal agencies to provide internships for students in pursuit of their major areas of study. The Office of the Secretary of Defense (OSD) has participated in this program since 1978.

Qualifications

Third- or fourth-year college undergraduates or graduate students are eligible. Applicants must undergo a security-clearance process that takes three to four months before starting the assignment. Applications are circulated within OSD. If an office is interested in an applicant, the candidate is contacted to begin the security clearance process.

Internship Dates and Duration

Duration covers a school semester or a summer session, usually from six weeks to three months.

Funding/Academic Credit

No stipends or benefits are available. School credit is strictly between students and their school.

To Apply

Four to five months before hoping to start an internship, the applicant should submit a letter from her school verifying enrollment and a Standard Form 171.

Women at DoD

No information available.

Contact Person

Carol R. Crook, Internship Coordinator; U.S. Department of Defense, Washington HQ Services, Room 3B347, Pentagon, Washington, DC 20301; (202) 697-7173.

U.S. Department of Defense, Office of the General Counsel

Rm 3E999
Pentagon
Washington, DC 20301-1600
(202) 695-3657

Organization Type and Purpose

OGC, the senior legal organization in the Department of Defense, provides advice to policymakers in the department. OGC also works with attorneys from other military departments and governmental agencies. Approximately 32 attorneys are on staff.

Internships

OGC offers a summer associates program for law school students. Associates serve as legal assistants, working closely with attorneys.

Qualifications

Candidates must be law students.

Internship Dates and Duration

The internship program is offered in the summer only.

Funding/Academic Credit

No information available.

To Apply

Contact the Office of Assistant General Counsel (International) at address below.

Women at OGC

No information available.

Contact Person

Paul Koffsky, Director of Internships; Office of the Assistant General Counsel, U.S. Department of Defense, Room 3E999, Pentagon, Washington, DC 20301-1600; (202) 695-3657.

U.S. Department of State

Recruitment Division
P.O. Box 12209
Arlington, VA 22209
(703) 875-7189

Organization Type and Purpose

The State Department is the U.S. agency responsible for handling foreign affairs for the federal government. The department maintains diplomatic relations worldwide with more than 230 embassies and consulates.

Internships

The department sponsors internships designed to encourage students to consider a career in foreign affairs. Interns are assigned to junior-level duties that may include research, correspondence, analyzing international issues, and work on cases related to domestic and international law. Most internships are located in Washington; however, a few openings exist in U.S. embassies abroad.

Qualifications

Undergraduates with junior standing and graduate students are eligible. Applicants must be U.S. citizens pursuing academic studies relevant to the office of interest and able to pass a background security check.

Internship Dates and Duration

Positions are available year-round; the typical internship lasts for one semester or the summer and is done on a full-time basis.

Funding/Academic Credit

Certain summer interns receive remuneration. Work-study interns, who are unpaid, serve for one semester or quarter during the year.

To Apply

Contact the internship coordinator for an application package. Return the application, with SF-171, a certified copy of academic transcripts, two letters of faculty recommendation, and a 500- to 775-word autobiography. Deadlines: for summer, November 1; for fall, March 1; for spring, June 30. When application is completed, it is sometimes helpful to contact directly the bureau(s) in which you are interested.

Women at the Department of State

Women comprise almost 40 percent of the department's work force. In the Foreign Service, however, less than 30 percent of employees are women.

Contact Person

Carol Mastriani, Intern Coordinator; U.S. Department of State, Recruitment Division, P.O. Box 12209, Arlington, VA 22209; (703) 875-7189.

U.S. General Accounting Office

National Recruitment Program
441 G Street NW, Room 4650
Washington, DC 20548
(202) 275-6092

Organization Type and Purpose

The GAO was created by the Congress as an independent, nonpartisan agency to assist in congressional oversight of the executive branch of the federal government. The office mainly audits and evaluates federal programs and reports its findings to Congress. GAO also has a national security and international affairs division where a broad range of U.S. national and international programs are covered.

Internships

GAO offers annual summer internships in public policy, accounting, and computer science. Public policy interns help examine the effectiveness of existing or proposed federal programs. These culminate in reports both to Congress and to the heads of federal agencies. Interns' on-the-job experience is supplemented by a comprehensive three-day training course.

Qualifications

Interns must be U.S. citizens. Public policy interns must be currently enrolled in a full-time graduate program in public policy, public health, or international affairs and have completed at least one year of graduate study.

Internship Dates and Duration

Internships are offered only during the summer on a full-time basis.

Funding/Academic Credit

Public policy interns are hired at the GS-7 level, or $1,530 per month; accounting and computer science interns at the GS-4 level.

To Apply

An application package must be submitted by March 19 with the following: GAO Form 129, a one-page essay, a letter of recommendation from the dean or faculty chair of your graduate school, and GAO Form 74 (voluntary). Contact GAO for specific information and forms.

Women at GAO

No information available.

Contact Person

Daena Morgan, Summer Internship Coordinator; U.S. General Accounting Office, National Recruitment Program, 441 G Street NW, Room 4650, Washington, DC 20548; (202) 275-6092.

Washington Office on Latin America

110 Maryland Avenue NE
Suite 404
Washington, DC 20002
(202) 544-8045

Organization Type and Purpose

WOLA was founded in 1974 to monitor human rights and political developments in Central and South America and to track the formulation and implementation of U.S. policies toward that region. WOLA sponsors seminars in which prominent Latin Americans address current issues. This office also publishes pamphlets and several newsletters, including *Latin American Update* and *Washington in Focus.*

Internships

Internships are available to undergraduates specializing in Latin American studies. Interns help organize conferences, receptions, and briefings; they run errands, cover hearings, and perform clerical duties.

Qualifications

Candidates must be undergraduate students in Latin American studies.

Internship Dates and Duration

Internships usually cover a semester period.

Funding/Academic Credit

Positions are unpaid.

To Apply

Contact the office manager.

Women at WOLA

No information available.

Contact Person

Coletta Youngers, Associate; Washington Office on Latin America, 110 Maryland Avenue NE, Suite 404, Washington, DC 20002; (202) 544-8045.

Women's Action for Nuclear Disarmament

P.O. Box 153
New Town Branch
Boston, MA 02258
(617) 643-6740

Washington Office:
305 Seventh Street SE, Suite 204
Washington, DC 20003
(212) 543-8505

Organization Type and Purpose

WAND is a nonprofit advocacy organization seeking to prevent nuclear war by providing information, educational materials, and training about nuclear weapons issues to the public. It actively lobbies for arms control legislation and reduced military spending.

Internships

Interns lobby, participate in strategy meetings, answer inquiries, deliver literature to congressional offices, and help produce publications. They attend hearings and observe key congressional votes and debates on arms control legislation. Interns are encouraged to initiate special projects. The WAND staff is committed to work with interns to ensure that their contribution of time and energy will afford them a valuable and comprehensive work experience, with the expectation they will make a substantial contribution to our organization.

Qualifications

WAND prefers undergraduates or graduates who are willing to work for more than three months. It is helpful if the applicant has related experience through either course work or campus activities.

Internship Dates and Duration

Internships are year-round, for approximately three months or longer.

Funding/Academic Credit

The internships are not funded, but academic credit may be obtained.

To Apply

Apply two to three months before desired period of internship. If not applying through a program such as the Washington Center (see "Special Internship Programs"), send a resume and writing sample. WAND will also interview candidates.

Women at WAND

Of staff and interns, 90 percent are women.

Contact Person

Suzy Kerr, Political Director; Women's Action for Nuclear Disarmament, 305 Seventh Street SE, Suite 204, Washington, DC 20003; (202) 543-8505; in Boston, call (617) 643-6740.

World Bank Summer Employment Program

1818 H Street NW
Washington, DC 20433
(202) 477-3421 or (202) 477-1234

Organization Type and Purpose

The World Bank, formally known as the International Bank for Reconstruction and Development, is an international institution founded to promote economic development. Its multinational staff and headquarters are located in Washington, DC.

Internships

The summer program is open to full-time, degree-seeking graduate students on a worldwide basis and attracts a large number of highly qualified candidates. Of approximately 2,000 applications received annually, only 120-140 are selected. Students typically undertake analytical research and computer work under senior staff guidance.

Qualifications

Candidates must have at least a bachelor's degree (or equivalent), be enrolled in a degree program in the spring, and returning to additional full-time studies in the fall. They also should have a solid academic background in economics, finance, accounting, statistics, or computer science, with some relevant work experience in their field. English proficiency is required. Other languages such as French, Spanish, Arabic, Chinese, or Portuguese are sometimes required.

Internship Dates and Duration

The internship covers the summer months from June to September.

Funding/Academic Credit

A monthly salary is paid, but successful candidates must provide their own transportation and accommodations.

To Apply

The deadline is February 28. Applicants will be notified by April or May if selected and by late May or June if not. Contact the bank for the Summer Programs application form, which must be mailed by deadline date. The summer program is not a means of entry into the bank.

Women at the World Bank

No information available.

Contact Person

Summer Employment Program Coordinator; World Bank, 1818 H Street NW, Washington, DC 20433; (202) 477-3421 or (202) 477-1234.

FOUR

Special Internship Programs

FEDERAL GOVERNMENT INTERNSHIPS

Federal Government Cooperative Education (Co-op) Program

Many federal government agencies offer cooperative education programs in which college students divide their time between the classroom and a salaried government job. Over 900 colleges and universities in the United States currently participate in federal co-op programs. The participating federal agencies with positions relevant for students interested in international security include the Department of Commerce, the Department of Defense; intelligence organizations, including the Central Intelligence Agency and the National Security Agency; the Department of State; and the Army, Navy, and Air Force.

Students can arrange to work half-day and attend classes half-day to fulfill their commitment, or work full time one semester and attend classes full time the next. (For more information, see the booklet *Earn and Learn: Cooperative Education Opportunities,* listed in the section on "Internship Directories.")

Presidential Management Internship Program

Coordinator, Presidential Management Internship Program
Office of Personnel Management
1900 E Street NW
Washington, DC 20415
(202) 632-6276

The Presidential Management Intern Program provides a special means of entry into the federal service for recipients of graduate degrees who have demonstrated an interest in the management or analysis of public policies or programs. Each year, a limited number of interns will receive two-year appointments, unless a third year is approved, to developmental positions in the federal government. Offers of employment are made by participating agencies to individuals desiring experience in a variety of functional areas as well as those with specific management interests. The program selects finalists from an appropriate pool. For further information, please contact the coordinator.

AGENCIES THAT ARRANGE INTERNSHIPS

A few third-party organizations act as intermediaries in arranging an internship. Two of these organizations are listed below:

Washington Center

514 Tenth Street NW
Suite 600
Washington, DC 20004
(202) 289-8680

The Washington Center is a nonprofit educational organization founded in 1975. The center provides symposia and internships in the Washington area to interested students in a variety of fields. Full-time internships are supplemented by weekly academic seminars in this program. Internships are with independent sector organizations, including nonprofit organizations, advocacy groups, membership associations, and foundations. The internships carry a stipend of $1,000, and the student is expected to prepare an essay of publishable quality and a speech on a topic related to the independent sector and the student's internship experience.

Washington Internships Unlimited

4264 South 35th Street
Arlington, VA 22206
(703) 820-3523

Washington Internships Unlimited operates an internship service especially for women. WIU's counseling helps the prospective intern to find a position available in her area of interest, define the goals of her internship, prepare a strong resume, make the best impression in interviews, and get the most out of the internship experience.

FIVE

Internship Directories

Directory of Career Resources for Women. Alvin Renetzky, ed. Santa Monica, CA: Ready Reference Press, 1979. $47.50.
—To order: Send requests to P.O. Box 5249, Santa Monica, CA 90405. Do not send payment in advance.

This directory concentrates on organizations offering services such as job referral, career counseling, reentry programs, and continuing education. Entries include general information about the organization (e.g., address and telephone number), description of services offered, and service fees (if any). A listing of federal job information centers is included.

The entries are listed alphabetically by sponsoring organization and are indexed by subject and geographical location.

Directory of Financial Aid for Women 1985–1986, 3d ed. Gail Ann Schlachter, ed. Coral Springs, FL: B. Klein Publications, 1985. $40.00.
—To order: Contact the publisher: telephone (305) 752-1708; address: P.O. Box 8503, Coral Springs, FL 33065.

This biennial directory lists financial-aid programs open exclusively to women from high school through postdoctoral levels. The awards are divided into five categories: scholarships, fellowships, grants, awards, and paid internships.

Each entry provides the sponsoring organization's name, address, and telephone number. Other information includes the purpose of the financial-aid program, the award's monetary value and special nonfunded features of the program, duration of the award, qualification requirements, program limitations, and application deadline.

All areas of the sciences, social sciences, and humanities are covered. The entries are indexed by program title, sponsoring organization, geographical location, subject, and application deadline. An annotated bibliography of general financial aid directories is included.

Directory of Internships, Work Experience Programs, and On-the-Job Training Opportunities, 2d ed., two vols. Alvin Renetzky, ed. Santa Monica, CA: Ready Reference Press, 1976. $95.00 for set.
—To order: Send requests to P.O. Box 5249, Santa Monica, CA: 90405. Do not send payment in advance.

Unlike many others, this directory offers more than simply a listing of internships with nonprofit peace organizations. It lists opportunities in more than 250 subject areas, many of them touching on some aspect of security. However, it is more than 10 years old.

Some 500 organizations offering internships or off-campus study opportunities to individuals at high school through postdoctoral levels are included. Entries provide title of the training program, a brief job description, the number of positions available, the requirements, type of compensation, information on stipulations or special features, and the application procedure. (Neither organization address nor a contact person is listed.)

Directory of Public Service Internships: Opportunities for the Graduate, Post-Graduate, and Mid-Career Professional. Jane C. Kendall and Elizabeth Y. Coppedge, eds. Washington, DC: National Society for Internships and Experiential Education, 1979.
—To order: The directory may be available in libraries, but it has been subsumed by the National Directory of Internships (listed below) and is no longer in print.

Approximately 150 internships and fellowship opportunities are listed predominately for graduate, postgraduate, and mid-career professionals; some programs accept undergraduate students. Entries include address and phone number of the sponsoring organization, as well as the name of the contact person. There is a brief history of each organization. Also detailed are sources of funding and the number of interns accepted annually.

Listings provide program design and objectives, selection procedures, geographical placement of the interns, method of compensation, and eligibility requirements. Each entry specifies program duration, which generally ranges from one month to two years.

Internships and fellowships are indexed by 13 broad career headings. Most listings in the governmental category are in local, state, or federal legislative branches; of the very few related to security, those are in nonprofit peace organizations. These entries are cross-indexed by subject and indexed alphabetically and geographically. The directory also provides a list of clearinghouses.

Directory of Special Opportunities for Women. Martha Merrill Doss, ed. Garrett Park, MD: Garrett Park Press, 1981. $18.00 prepaid; $19.00 if billed.
—To order: Contact the Garrett Park Press, P.O. Box 190, Garrett Park, MD 20896; or call (301) 946-2553.

This directory describes various resources that would be valuable to women entering or reentering the work force, especially in nontraditional careers (those in which women comprise 25 percent or less of the work force). It lists not only internships, but also educational opportunities, formal networks, and sources of peer counseling and professional information.

The first section contains an alphabetical listing of national organizations, associations, programs, and governmental agencies established as resources for women. Section two—indexed by state and divided into zip code zones—contains women's centers, study programs, and resource agencies; city, state, and county commissions on the status of women; local YWCA programs; and other private and governmental organizations. The final two sections comprise listings of women's colleges in the United States, publishing companies, grant-making foundations, and networking organizations for women.

Directory of Washington Internships: A Guide to Current Internship Programs and Placements in the Nation's Capital, 1983–84 ed. National Center for Public Service Internship Programs, 1983.
—To order: Out of print, but may be in some libraries.

This biennial directory lists approximately 140 internships in Washington, DC, most of which are for undergraduate and graduate students (some programs will accept "highly motivated" high school students). Each entry provides address and telephone number of the administering agency.

Internship information includes purpose and duration of the program, number of interns accepted, responsibilities and qualifications, and the application procedure. The opportunities vary in terms of duration and level of intern responsibility.

Internships are categorized under 20 career headings; 2 cover security studies—government/public policy and international affairs. These sections offer a variety of security-related internships and though short may prove valuable.

An index of sponsoring organizations is provided.

Earn and Learn: Cooperative Education Opportunities, 1989–90 ed. Joseph M. Re, ed. Alexandria, VA: Octameron Associates, Inc., 1988. 30 pp. $3.00, plus $1.25 shipping.
—To order: Send check or money order to Octameron Associates, P.O. Box 3437, Alexandria, VA 22302; or order by phone: (703) 823-1882.

This booklet is devoted exclusively to co-op opportunities in the federal government. It not only lists the government agencies that offer cooperative educational programs to students, but also lists the colleges and universities in each state that participate in such programs. There are cooperative opportunities for students in associate, baccalaureate, and graduate degree programs.

A particularly useful feature of the directory is the section on "Best Bets," which lists the agencies with the most promising opportunities based on an individual's field of interest and educational level.

While the booklet is helpful and informative, it includes some misinformation about internships with the federal government. Many paid internships have become unpaid positions in recent years due to the restrictions imposed by the budget deficit.

The Experienced Hand: A Student Manual for Making the Most of an Internship. Timothy Stanton and Kamil Ali, eds. Cranston, RI: Carroll Press, 1982. $8.95.

—To order: Send a check or money order to Carroll Press, P.O. Box 8113, Cranston, RI 02920; telephone number: (401) 942-1587.

Getting Work Experience: The Students' Directory of Professional Internship Programs That Lead to Careers. Betsy Bauer, ed. New York: Dell Publishers, 1985.

—To order: Out of print, but may be in some libraries.

This directory lists about 10,000 summer internships for undergraduate students. Each entry describes the organization, providing an address and in most cases a telephone number. Internship data include the number and kind of positions being offered, qualification requirements, type of compensation (usually academic credit), and the application procedure. Most appointments are offered during the college summer break.

Internships are categorized under 11 career field headings; they are primarily geared to undergraduate students. The majority of the government-related, entry-level positions are with local or state legislatures, and a number of opportunities exist also in peace organizations. All entries are indexed geographically and alphabetically.

Guide to Careers and Graduate Education in Peace Studies. Daniel C. Thomas, ed. Amherst, MA: Five College Program in Peace and World Security Studies at Hampshire College, 1987. $3.50.

—To order: Send a check or money order—payable to the Trustees of Hampshire College—to the Five College Program in Peace and World Security Studies, c/o Hampshire College, Amherst, MA 01002.

This guide details only a handful of available fellowships and internships, but it does contain a list of organizations in the arms control and security fields (with addresses and phone numbers). In addition, there is a section on career options open to those interested in peace studies, with brief descriptions of both traditional (law) and not-so-traditional (mediation and conflict resolution) fields.

The guide also contains a listing of graduate and law school programs relevant to international security.

Guide to Careers in World Affairs. New York: Foreign Policy Association, 1987. 300 pp. plus. $10.95, plus $1.75 shipping.

—To order: Send check or money order, made payable to the Foreign Policy Association, 729 Seventh Avenue, 8th Floor, New York, NY 10019.

This volume contains chapters on careers in the international arena— in business, consulting, finance and banking, law, and journalism. Other chapters deal with careers in teaching; translating and interpreting; nonprofit organizations; the federal government; and multilateral organizations such as the United Nations. Each chapter lists several organizations in the field, with addresses and information on basic hiring practices and organizational philosophy.

Most entries contain a brief mention about internships; in addition, there is a special section on internships in categories similar to those listed above. While it only scratches the surface of available opportunities, it could be a good starting point.

International Directory for Youth Internships with the United Nations, Its Specialized Agencies and Nongovernmental Organizations, 1984–1985. Cynthia Morehouse, ed. New York: New Horizons Press, 1984. $4.75, plus $2.50 shipping.

—To order: Send check or money order to New Horizons Press, Suite 9A, 777 United Nations Plaza, New York, NY 10017; or order by phone: (212) 972-9877.

The Internship Experience. Lynne Schaefer Gross, ed. Prospect Heights, IL: Waveland Press, 1987. $8.95.
—To order: Send requests to Waveland Press, P.O. Box 400, Prospect Heights, IL 60079; or call (312) 634-0081. Do not send payment in advance.

This book provides the student with "a practical guide to the general procedures and practices of student internships." Primarily concerned with the media, the book is most useful to students pursuing opportunities in radio, television, film, advertising, or journalism, but much of the information is of general use. Suggestions for resumes and cover letters are included, as well as an overview chapter outlining what a student can hope to accomplish through the internship experience.

Internships and Fellowships: Congressional, Federal, and Other Work Experience Opportunities. Betsy Reifsnyder, ed. Congressional Research Service Report No. 87-237C. Washington, DC: Library of Congress, May 1987. 15 pp. No charge.
—To order: You must order the report through a member of Congress. Call your representative's local office for more information.

This CRS report provides useful information on how to apply for internships with members of Congress or with congressional committees. In addition to tips on applying to an office directly, it details programs that place interns in congressional offices. These include the Lyndon Baines Johnson Internship Program and programs run by universities and nonprofit organizations.

The report also briefly outlines internship opportunities in government agencies other than Congress and provides information on congressional, judicial, and presidential fellowships that place individuals in congressional or executive branch offices. The information includes addresses and telephone numbers for the sponsoring organization, as well as a brief description of the program.

An annotated bibliography lists sources valuable to the individual looking for an internship. In addition to bibliographic listings, the text of the report mentions resources like the *Congressional Directory,* the *Congressional Staff Directory,* the *Congressional Yellow Book,* and the *Federal Yellow Book;* all may be useful for deciding whom to contact in pursuing an internship and are available in most libraries.

Invest Yourself: A Catalogue of Volunteer Opportunities. New York: Commission on Voluntary Service and Action, 1982.
—To order: Out of print, but may be available in some libraries.

The catalogue lists many opportunities for those interested in volunteer work during the summer months. Most listings are for local impact programs, although some take the intern outside of the continental United States and others may be pertinent for students interested in national security from a peace perspective. None of the internships are funded, and a few programs have associated costs, in some cases, in excess of $1,500.

Entries provide the geographic area of the program, general information, contact person, address, and telephone number. Agencies offering summer positions are specially marked, and the listings are cross-referenced for students under 18, international placements, summer placements, and types of skills needed.

National Directory of Internships. Raleigh, NC: National Society for Internships and Experiential Education, 1987. $20.00, plus $2.50 shipping.
—To order: Send check or money order to the National Society for Internships and Experiential Education, 3509 Haworth Drive, Suite 207, Raleigh, NC 27609; or order by phone at (919) 787-3263.

This biennial directory lists approximately 500 internship opportunities available to high-school, undergraduate, or graduate students, as well as experienced professionals. Entries include the address and telephone number for the sponsoring organization and the name of the contact person. Other information provides a brief job description, duration of the program, number of interns accepted, eligibility requirements, and application procedure. Few entries discuss compensation.

Internships are grouped into 11 general fields, such as government and public policy, education, and business and finance. Of the nearly 81 listings under government and public policy, the majority are in local legislatures, political grass-roots organizations, and private, nonprofit peace groups.

All entries are indexed alphabetically and geographically. The book also includes a list of clearinghouses that refer or place students with various agencies.

National Register of Internships & Experiential Education: A Guide to Off-Campus Study Programs and Opportunities. Ross C. Lewchuk, ed. Washington, DC: Acropolis Books Ltd., 1973. $3.95.
—To order: Call Acropolis Books at (202) 387-6805. A credit-card order will be processed within 24 hours.

This register is actually a report on the general state of internships and other off-campus study opportunities. However, the book does list organizations that have off-campus study opportunities or are interested in developing them. These organizations offer internships in numerous fields, including government and public policy, economics, and education.

Most of the security-related internships are in government, political science, and sociology departments at various colleges and universities. However, there is only a list of the organizations, so it is not always possible to identify the nature of the work the intern will be assigned. Nevertheless, for interns who wish to work on a college campus, this book will be helpful.

1989 Internships: 38,000 On-the-Job Training Opportunities for College Students and Adults. Katherine Jobst, ed. Cincinnati, OH: F&W Publications, 1989. $21.95, plus $2.50 shipping.

—To order: Send a check or money order to F&W Publications at 1507 Dana Avenue, Cincinnati, OH 45207; or order by phone: (513) 531-2222.

This directory lists 38,000 internships available to undergraduate or graduate students and nonstudents. Each entry includes a brief description of the sponsoring organization, with address, telephone number, and contact person; a basic job description; the number of positions available; compensation; eligibility requirements; application procedure; the number of applications received annually; and a description of benefits such as housing and travel when applicable.

The majority of internships listed under Government and Public Administration are in municipal or state government offices dealing with city planning, local legislatures, and public relations. The Public Interest/Public Service section lists a few nonprofit peace organizations with internships, but the directory does not list traditional security-related internships.

International internships and foreign applications to U.S. internships are also covered. The directory does not include those programs that offer internships only to persons enrolled in "very limited, exclusive educational or training programs," those that charge application fees exceeding $50, or organizations that offer a limited number of positions.

Entries are indexed alphabetically and geographically.

Peace & International Security Internships in the Washington, DC, Area. Washington, DC: ACCESS, A Security Information Service, 1988–89. $5.00, plus $1.00 shipping and handling.

—To order: Send check to ACCESS, 1730 M Street NW, Suite 605, Washington, DC 20036; or order by phone (202) 785-6630.

This publication lists organizations in the Washington area that at one time or another have had interns. Some have a formal application process while others have found their interns through an informal search. The directory lists each organization's name and address, its purpose, and its major issue areas. At the end of the listings is a bibliography of other internship directories and relevant publications.

Stopout! Working Ways to Learn. Joyce Slayton Mitchell, ed. Garrett Park, MD: Garrett Park Press, 1979. $7.95 prepaid; $8.95 billed.
—To order: Write Garrett Park Press, P.O. Box 190, Garrett Park, MD 20896; or phone (301) 946-2553.

This directory, aimed at postsecondary and undergraduate students, lists 137 volunteer and internship opportunities for students who defer higher education or take leave from school to work or study. Each entry gives address and telephone number of the sponsoring organization, as well as the person to contact. A detailed description of the organization includes its current projects and activities (e.g., publications), the number of permanent staff members, and its annual budget. Other information includes job description, qualification requirements, duration of the program, type of compensation, and application procedure. Most appointments are full time and vary in duration from one semester to one year.

The internships and volunteer positions are classified into nine broad career fields, which run the gamut from government to religious-sponsored opportunities. A small number of security-related opportunities appear under the headings government-sponsored agencies and women and minorities. These positions are generally in nonprofit peace organizations. Each listing is indexed alphabetically and geographically.

Storming Washington: An Intern's Guide to National Government. Washington, DC: American Political Science Association, 1986. 50 pp. $3.00, plus 50 cents for shipping.
—To order: Send check or money order to APSA, 1527 New Hampshire Avenue, NW, Washington, DC 20036. Orders must be prepaid; for information, call (202) 482-2512.

This small booklet contains useful information on tracking down an internship in the nation's capital and making the most of the opportunity once found. Sections include "Whom Do I Contact," "Selling Yourself," "Creating a Resume," and "Enhancing Your Chances." Appendixes provide listings of other internship directories, a guide to organized university programs, tips on finding temporary housing in the District of Columbia, and a brief rundown of other resources for political scientists in the area.

This directory is not especially helpful in locating internship opportunities; however, it can be useful in finding a job and is certainly worth the modest price.

Student Guide to Fellowships and Internships. Students of Amherst College, eds. New York: E.P. Dutton, 1980.
—To order: Out of print, but may be available in some libraries.

This book, aimed at undergraduates, is divided into two sections. The first provides general information on attaining internships and fellowships. The second section lists available internships and fellowship opportunities as of 1980.

Information on the sponsoring organization includes data on the requirements, duration of the program, compensation, fee (if any), number of positions offered, and application deadline. In addition, there is a section providing "inside" information by former interns with tips on getting accepted, the daily life, and other interesting features about the position.

Entries are listed alphabetically by sponsoring organization and indexed by both geographic location and subject.

Summer Jobs for 1989: Opportunities in the Federal Government. Washington, DC: United States Office of Personnel Management, Announcement 414, December 1988. No charge.
—To order: Phone the Office of Personnel Management in Washington (202) 653-8468. First there is a recorded message, but eventually an operator answers from whom you can order the book.

This booklet will be very useful for anyone interested in a summer job with the federal government. It includes a Standard Form 171 and a Supplemental Qualifications Statement; the former must be filled out by applicants for most federal jobs.

The booklet contains listings of government agencies, mainly in the executive branch, that offer summer positions. Many are clerical jobs that pay at low government salary levels (GS-1 through -4), but there are also positions for individuals with bachelor's degrees and, in some cases, graduate work or master's degrees. These positions carry a salary of GS-5 through -9, and many are relevant to those interested in global security and its composite fields, including economics, law, public administration, and international relations. Each listing includes the application deadline, salary level, and the areas of expertise relevant to the position; some listings briefly describe the position.

Other general information pertains to steps in applying for summer positions with the government. A list of addresses of recruitment offices for government agencies with summer programs is provided, as well as the addresses of the Office of Personnel Management's Federal Job Information and Testing Offices in each state.

Technology and Society Internship Directory: A Comprehensive Guide to Washington, DC, Internships. Washington, DC: Student Pugwash, 1987. $20.00; $10.00 for students; plus $2.00 postage.
—To order: Send check or money order to Student Pugwash, 1638 R Street, NW, Suite 32, Washington, DC 20009; or by phone, call (202) 328-6555.

Containing over 100 listings, this directory is a useful guide to opportunities and how best to pursue them. Many listings are relevant to security studies. Entries include comprehensive information on the sponsoring organization, including address, contact person, and institutional description. Also detailed are duties, work environment, dates of internship, compensation, qualifications, and application procedure associated with the position.

In addition to listings of organizational internship programs, the directory includes useful information on creating a resume, writing cover letters, and requesting letters of recommendation. There are also sections of general advice for interns and ideas for creating internships.

The volume is cleverly designed for easy use. Symbols on every page indicate the type of organization, and easily visible keywords reveal the location of the program, type of compensation, work environment, dates of the internship, and qualifications at a glance. Organizations are indexed alphabetically.

Appendix A
SAMPLE RESUME

Jane Doe
1000 Fiction Street
Washington DC 20001
(202) 444-1212

EDUCATION

B.A., Fictitious University, College Town, VA, expected May 1991. Major in international relations. Distinguished Alumni Award, Phelps Award. Courses included

- America and the World
- U.S.-Soviet Relations, 1945 to the Present
- Interdependence and the Third World
- Human Rights and International Politics
- International Economics
- The United States in Latin America

High school diploma, Walt Whitman High School, Springs, IL. Graduated 1987. National Merit Scholar.

WORK EXPERIENCE

Administrative Assistant, Office of the Dean, Fictitious University. September 1988 to May 1989. Provided general office assistance, including word processing, maintaining admissions records on a computer filing system, and writing articles for alumni publication.

Retail Salesperson, Hampshire Nursery, Springs, IL. June to August 1988 and June to August 1987. Advised customers on plant selection and care.

ACTIVITIES

Students and International Security (SIS), Fictitious University. Established this student organization concerned with international security issues and their impact on students. Served as president 1987–88 and 1988–89. SIS sponsored several forums to encourage campus wide discussion of such issues as apartheid, the environment and security, and the role of Congress in policy-making.

International Relations Club, Fictitious University. Member since 1987. Participated in simulation of international crisis in Persian Gulf.

Track team, Fictitious University. September 1987 to present. Participate in cross-country races.

TRAVEL/LANGUAGES

Have traveled in Western Europe and Mexico, and speak conversational Spanish.

Appendix B
SAMPLE COVER LETTER

March 15, 1989

Ms. Frances Burwell
Executive Director
Women In International Security
School of Public Affairs
University of Maryland
College Park, MD 20742

Dear Ms. Burwell,

I am very interested in working as an intern for the Women In International Security program during the summer of 1989. My resume is enclosed, but I would like to introduce myself briefly and explain why I am applying and what I think I could contribute to WIIS.

I am enrolled as a junior at Fictitious University, majoring in international affairs with an emphasis on security studies. In addition to fulfilling the course requirements for my major, I also founded a student organization on campus to focus on current security issues of concern to students. We have held a number of campuswide forums and debates on subjects ranging from arms control to South Africa and human rights. I was gratified to see a number of women in the audience, often more than 50 percent of the attendance. I would like to encourage more women to transform an academic interest in international security into a rewarding career. I understand this is one of your organization's primary goals, and I would like to be a part of that process.

As my resume indicates, I have written a number of papers on various national security themes, ranging from conventional stability in Europe to the current peace plan in Central America. I eventually hope to pursue these interests in graduate school. Meanwhile, I am trying to gain as much experience and exposure as possible in the security field. I was fortunate in receiving a scholarship to travel to Washington, DC, to attend a seminar for women interested in this area. That experience was not only broadening, but it also encouraged me to think about the roles that women have traditionally had in the security arena.

All this leads to my interest in working for WIIS. I think I could be useful in several ways: my work on campus has given me solid organizational skills that I think would be of benefit; I enjoy writing and research and would be delighted to undertake any projects that may be gathering dust on your shelves; I am strongly committed to helping women pursue their interests in security-related fields; and I could act as a link between WIIS and the student community.

Sincerely,

Jane Doe
1000 Fiction Street
Washington, DC 20001

Enclosure
Telephone: (202) 444-1212

Appendix C
SAMPLE REQUEST FOR A LETTER OF RECOMMENDATION

March 15, 1989

Dr. Elizabeth Blum
Department of Political Science
Fictitious University
College Town, VA 22033

Dear Dr. Blum,

I am writing to ask if you would write a brief letter on my behalf. I am applying to the Department of State for a 10-week internship to begin in June 1989. I hope to pursue a career in government upon completing my master's degree, and firsthand experience with the governmental, bureaucratic process would be invaluable.

I would appreciate your stressing my interest in NATO, as I am applying to the Bureau of European and Canadian Affairs. As you know, I have done research and written many papers on NATO issues. I think that my academic work and my backround as a research assistant will enhance my performance as an intern.

A stamped, addressed envelope is enclosed. I would appreciate it if you could send it before April 1, 1989. If you have any questions or comments, I can be reached at (202)444-1212. Many thanks in advance for your help.

Sincerely,

Jane Doe
1000 Fiction Street
Washington, DC 20001

INDEX

ALPHABETICAL LIST OF ORGANIZATIONS

ISSUE ORIENTATION OF ORGANIZATION

Arms Control

Asia

Economics and Trade

General

Human Rights

TYPE OF ORGANIZATION

Center for International Security Studies at Maryland

The Center for International Security Studies at Maryland is a scholarly organization dedicated to interdisciplinary research, education, and publication in the field of international security and foreign policy. Through rigorous analysis and an emphasis on excellence in education and training, CISSM seeks to make a contribution to the evolving international dialogue on the complex challenges of achieving peace and security in the 1990s.

Founded in 1984, the Center is located at the University of Maryland's School of Public Affairs. Each year the Center invites a multinational group of scholars to study at College Park. These graduate and postdoctoral fellows work on a variety of research projects. CISSM also involves students enrolled in master's and doctorate degree programs in public management, government and politics, and several other fields.

Along with its core activities, CISSM hosts three major projects:

Economics and National Security, an interdisciplinary research and teaching project which examines the relationship between national security and economic issues. The program has developed several new courses, presented lectures and research workshops, and sponsored fellowships.

The **Nuclear History Program,** a multinational research project which explores the role of nuclear weapons in postwar relationships among the United States, the Soviet Union, and Western Europe. NHP involves university faculty and staff as well as research teams from the United Kingdom, West Germany, and France. As the American base of the NHP, CISSM is active in research, publications, seminars, and conferences.

Women In International Security, a national, nonpartisan network and professional development group for women working in foreign policy and defense. WIIS runs a computerized databank, which allows women to be matched with suitable professional opportunities, and sponsors a series of seminars and other programs. (For further information, see the next page.)

To receive information on CISSM and the above projects, please indicate the material desired below, supply your name and address, and mail this form to: **CISSM, Morrill Hall, University of Maryland, College Park, MD 20742; telephone (301) 454-4344.**

☐ Please send information on CISSM.

☐ Please send a listing of CISSM publications and an order form.

☐ Please send information on the Economics and National Security Program.

☐ Please send information on the Nuclear History Program.

☐ Please send information on Women In International Security.

Name: ______________________________

Address: ______________________________

____

Daytime phone: ______________________________

Women In International Security

Women In International Security is a national network and professional development program dedicated to enhancing the career prospects of women working on international issues. It includes women in academia and the military, in the policy-making and nonprofit communities, and in the research and business sectors. WIIS (pronounced "wise") provides women with a structure that encourages the creation of informal links and continuing career contacts. It is also a clearinghouse on information for and about women working on these vital issues.

WIIS sponsors a number of specific activities designed to help women prosper in their careers, including:

The **WIIS Databank,** a computerized database that matches women with professional opportunities. It has been used to compile invitation lists for conferences and seminars, identify speakers and members of commissions, find possible job applicants, and announce relevant workshops and research opportunities.

The **WIIS Directories,** of which this publication is the first. Two others are underway: one on midcareer programs and fellowships, and a second on various organizations and resources for women working in this field.

WIIS Words, the newsletter of the project. Serving as an essential link between the many women involved in WIIS, it describes the activities sponsored by the program, as well as encouraging the exchange of information and highlighting the achievements of women.

The **WIIS Seminars,** which bring together women for wide-ranging discussions of substantive issues and professional development strategies.

Initiated in July 1987 with a grant from the Ford Foundation, WIIS is run under the auspices of the Center for International Security Studies at Maryland, directed by Catherine McArdle Kelleher. CISSM is located at the School of Public Affairs of the University of Maryland at College Park.

To receive further information on WIIS, please fill out the form below and mail it to: Women In International Security, CISSM, Morrill Hall, University of Maryland, College Park, MD 20742; telephone (301) 454-5057.

☐ Please send information in WIIS.

☐ Please send a questionnaire, so that I can be included in the WIIS databank.

Name: ______________________________

Address: ______________________________

____

Daytime phone: ______________________________